WO[illegible] HE

Other books in Target by the same author:

DETECTIVE WORZEL GUMMIDGE
WORZEL GUMMIDGE AND THE RAILWAY SCARECROWS
EARTHY MANGOLD AND WORZEL GUMMIDGE

WORZEL GUMMIDGE AT THE CIRCUS

BARBARA EUPHAN TODD

TARGET

A TARGET BOOK
published by
the Paperback Division of
W. H. ALLEN & Co. Ltd

A Target Book
Published in 1980
by the Paperback Division of W. H. Allen & Co. Ltd
A Howard & Wyndham Company
44 Hill Street, London W1X 8LB

This edition first published by Evans Brothers Ltd in 1970
Adapted from the original edition published 1956

To Osyth Leeston 'stands to reason'

Frontispiece illustration by Jill Crockford

Printed in Great Britain by
Richard Clay (The Chaucer Press), Ltd.,
Bungay, Suffolk

ISBN 0 426 20128 0

1 The Red-letter Morning

'Does a red-letter day come once in a blue moon?' asked Robin. His school teacher had told him that a red-letter day was a very special one, and he knew that blue moons were rare.

His Aunt Ruby was too busy to answer. She was bustling about the kitchen of Station Cottage, which had a front door that opened on to the platform. Every now and then, she stopped to cram something – a packet of cornflakes and an egg-whisk, a box of matches and a mouse-trap – into a bag that was already much too full. She was wearing her Sunday clothes and hat, and her gloves and purse were on the kitchen table.

'You never know what you may need,' she muttered. 'You never know what you may need when you're going to help other people to move house.'

The other people were Robin's parents, who were leaving the house and the greengrocer's shop in London, and were coming to Scatterbrook to grow vegetables.

'Mum and Dad aren't moving the *house*,' argued Robin. 'They're only moving the furniture and things into Finch Cottage.'

'That reminds me, you'll need this.' Aunt Ruby opened a drawer, took out a key, and handed it to Robin. 'I want you to open all the cottage windows on fine mornings, and shut them again every evening or if it rains. We can't be too careful not to let the place get damp or your Dad will be ill again.'

If anything were needed to turn a red-letter day into brightest scarlet – the most glorious colour in the paint-box – it was the feeling of that key.

Everything was so exciting that he spun a tin of floor polish on the kitchen table, just for the joy of watching it whizz round. He would have liked to whizz himself. Not only was his Aunt Ruby going away for a whole week, and leaving him in the care of his uncle, who was a very unfussy sort of man, and out all day because of his work on the railways, but the larder was full of cooked pasties, apple-turnovers, tomatoes, cheese, bananas, oranges – all the things needed for picnic meals that needed no washing up afterwards. Not only was Mildew Turmut, the railway scarecrow, busy on the Station allotment, but Worzel Gummidge, Earthy Mangold, Hannah, the invalid scarecrow, and Bessie, the one-horned cow, were in a near-by field. Not only was it Saturday morning, and a whole holiday, but the key in Robin's pocket would open the door of the cottage that was to be his very own home as soon as Aunt Ruby had helped his parents to move from London.

'Can I sleep there?' he asked.

'Sleep where, I should like to know?' Aunt Ruby snatched up the tin of polish and stuffed it into her bulging bag.

'In Finch Cottage to keep it aired.'

'The very idea with no furniture in the place! You'll sleep here in your own bed, and do what your uncle tells you *if* he remembers to tell you anything. Look out of the window, there's a good boy, and see if the train's coming.'

Robin looked, not along the shining rails, so soon to be reburnished by the wheels of a fussy little train, but across them to where Mildew Turmut, only sister of the scarecrow, Worzel Gummidge, was waving her red and green flags to scare white butterflies from the cabbages. Her horse-hair plaits (once the stuffing of a carriage seat) were dangling against the scarf embroidered with the words *British Railways*. He could not see the crimson lettering but he knew it was there, to add to the joy of his own particular red-letter day.

'There's one good thing about living on a station, it does give you extra time for packing,' said Aunt Ruby.

There was, thought Robin, more than one good thing about living in a cottage whose front door opened straight on to Scatterbrook platform. Then, as Mildew Turmut shambled forward, blew her whistle, and waved her red flag in a furious attempt to scare the train, he said, 'It's coming now,' and he craned his neck to watch the train.

In another few minutes, Aunt Ruby was packed into her carriage. Just for a moment or two, Robin felt forlorn because his aunt was so kind, even if she were a little too fussy sometimes. He ran through the little gateway that opened on to the dusty lane leading to Scatterbrook village.

Marlene Snooks was reading a notice pinned to the board outside Scatterbrook Post Office, which was her favourite place, particularly on Saturday mornings, when she often picked up scraps of silver paper or the sticky paper that borders stamps, or anything else to add to her collections of the odds and ends that 'might come in useful some day'. If she had not been a little girl she might have been a dustman. If she had not been a human, she might have been a jackdaw.

'Look!' said Marlene, as Robin jangled some pennies against the key in his pocket, 'just you look here!'

Standing side by side, the two children took it in turns to read out the words of the most exciting notice. (They were printed in red to match Robin's red-letter day.)

VISIT OF BILTONG'S GIANT CIRCUS

COUNTLESS ATTRACTIONS

FATTEST LADY IN THE WORLD

PERFORMING ELEPHANT

'If I could get some elephant hairs, I could make them into rings and bangles,' said Marlene. 'I could twist them up with bits of gold wire, and sell them. Elephant hairs are ever so lucky.'

Robin read on:

SEA-LION ACROBATS

SHOOTING GALLERY

PICK-ME-UP THE WORLD-FAMOUS DOCTOR

CHILD WONDERS

Robin stopped reading, and stared at the notice until Marlene prodded his arm with her sharp little fingers.

'We could be *Child Wonders*, you and I could,' she said. 'I'd like to be a *Child Wonder* and jump through a flaming hoop, and hear all the people clapping.'

'It doesn't say *when* it is.' Robin stared at the foot of the notice. A ragged edge showed how some of the paper had been torn away roughly. 'It doesn't say *where* it is.'

'I know where it is. It's on the recreation ground,' Marlene told him. 'I saw the merry-go-rounds and swing-boats and caravans and all sorts go by early this morning. Let's go now!'

'Yes, let's go,' said Robin.

A few caravans were dotted about on the recreation ground – a flat stretch of ground between the main road and a cluster of bushes and low trees that lay on the lowest slope of the Downs.

A litter of canvas and ropes, packing cases and poles lay near the road. Two or three tents had been put up near to some caravans. Ponies were cropping the grass, a lurcher dog licked itself, and another gnawed a bone. It was all rather dreary.

Before the children had time to cross the sun-scorched grass, they heard a voice asking a magic question – 'Are you the sea-lions?'

Standing at the entrance of the tent was an enormously fat woman. She wore a shortish red dress, showing legs so thick that Robin thought they must have been put on upside down, and felt rather sorry for her.

'Come here,' she shouted, and waved an immense arm. 'Come here, can't you?'

Marlene went first, and Robin followed. For a few seconds it seemed as though the Fat Lady of the Circus was as queer in the head as she was huge in the body, because she did not trouble to say 'good morning' but asked again, 'Are you the sea-lions?'

'Do we look like sea-lions?' Marlene put the question pertly.

The Fat Lady looked at them, and sighed.

'You mean to say you've not come with the sea-lions?'

Robin, wishing that he had come with the sea-lions, shook his head.

'There now!' The Fat Lady put her huge hands on to her immense hips, and sighed gustily. 'There now! Why couldn't you have said so straight off? Soon as I saw you, I said to myself, "There's the two from *Archie's Animal Academy*, the two that's expected with the sea-lions, to look after them". Can you look after sea-lions?'

There was a pause, and then Robin answered boldly, 'Yes!'

On a red-letter morning like this he felt that he could look after anything. He had kept mice, and they were wild animals. He had driven Bessy, the one-horned cow, from her meadow to the milking shed, and surely Bessy was as frisky as a sea-lion.

'Then you'd better find Biltong, and look sharp about it.' The Fat Lady yawned. 'Biltong's at the station, or should be by now. It's just like him to expect me to put it on whether I get my rest or not. You've got to keep putting it on, haven't you? Put it on, and sleep it on – that's my motto. Take care of the pounds, and the stones will take care of themselves.'

She yawned again, and waved a hand (a hand like a leg of mutton – a hand that had fingers as fat as sausages) towards the tent flap.

'I've got to have a snack now – a snack and a nap, a nap and a snack, that's the way to do it.'

'When does the circus begin?' asked Marlene.

'If I knew *that*, I'd start slimming, and earn my living telling fortunes. The tight-rope lady's come out in spots, and the clown's gone on strike, and Pick-me-up's got the tooth-ache.

He's willing enough, I'll say that for Pick-me-up, but you can't expect him to sell bottles of Cure-all with one side of his face the size of half a football, can you?'

She paused for breath, and then asked another question.

'Can you two do anything besides sea-lions?'

'Yes,' said Robin.

'Not tight-rope walkers, are you?' asked the Fat Lady. 'Not tumblers or tap-dancers or trapezists?'

Robin shook his head. He could tumble off a bicycle or a wall, none better, but he could not dance or do acrobatics on a trapeze.

'I could jump through hoops!' said Marlene.

For the second time that morning, she had a vision of herself galloping round the ring on a piebald pony, leaping from its back to jump through a blazing hoop, landing on pony-back again, galloping and leaping again. She would wear a pink frock with spangles, and she would have silver stars in her flowing hair.

'I could!' she said. 'I know I could!'

Had not Miss Dollit, who taught in Sunday School, said that *anybody* who tried hard enough could do *anything*?

The Fat Lady was shaking her head and making her double chins waggle.

'You'd never do for that,' she answered, 'not in Biltong's circus. You're too peaky-looking, and your hair's too scraggy.'

'I could frizz it out.'

Marlene tugged at a straggle of hair, but the Fat Lady yawned again. 'You'd better stick to the sea-lions,' she said. 'You'll find Biltong at the station, meeting the elephant they're sending from *Blake's Emporium*. They said it was small, but is it small enough? It's one thing or t'other in a circus. You've got to be extra thin or extra fat, extra daring or extra comic. There's no medium or middling in a circus. Now if this were the largest elephant in the world, we'd be all right. If it's just about dainty we'll be all wrong. That's what you and me's got to think about.'

The cosy warmth of her voice as she said 'you and me' made the children feel, just for a moment, as though they were a part of the circus. It did not matter when the flap of the tent hid the Fat Lady from sight. The brave brass of the merry-go-round glinted in the sunshine. Soon the grass would smell of wild animals. The roars of the sea-lions would mingle with the song of birds. There was an elephant at Scatterbrook station, and they were going to meet it. Anything might happen now.

As they turned into the station yard where the coal trucks were emptied and the giant crane worked, a familiar voice shouted, 'All tickets ready!'

Mildew Turmut, the railway scarecrow, strode towards them determinedly. She was dressed as usual in a blue serge skirt and a porter's jacket. Instead of a belt, she wore a window strap round her waist, and her sardine-tin shoes clattered on the ground.

'Such goin's on!' grumbled Mildew. 'Earthy's gone to fetch her veil. I told her widders used to wear 'em when trains first started running on rails, and she said she'd got to be dressed proper.'

'But she's not a widow,' argued Robin. 'She's Worzel Gummidge's wife.'

'That's what I told her when Worzel went to be a stowaway.' Mildew waved her green flag towards a truck, piled high with coal dust. 'But she said a stowawayed husband was the same as not having a husband.' Mildew waved her red flag in the same direction as the green one. 'That truck won't be moved till they've mended the buffer. Very second class, I call it, to stow away to see the world in a truck with a broken buffer. Worzel won't see Scatterbrook neither now that he's buried in coal dust. There's Earthy coming now.'

The railway scarecrow glanced crossly at Earthy Mangold, who had just come into the station yard, and now moved, in her familiar hopping way, towards the children.

Her bottle-straw boots showed familiarly from under her

sacking skirt. Her blue check apron, with a banana skin handkerchief peeping from its pocket, was round her waist. Her sacking cloak trailed from her shoulders, but her kindly face was hidden in swathes of crimson curtain netting.

'I told you she *would* fetch her veil,' muttered Mildew.

'But it's the colour of raspberry jam!' said Marlene.

' 'Course it is,' agreed Earthy, who had now come so close that one bottle-straw boot scraped against Robin's shoe. ' 'Course it is, seein' it's made from a bit of old curtain Mrs Kibbins used for strainin' her rasps for jam.'

'Have you seen a man from the circus – a man called Mr Biltong?'

'There *were* a man about,' said Mildew. 'Very second class he were, too. He'd a yellow weskitt, and a red handkercher tied round his neck. He'd a very second class cold, too, more like Cheap Day Excursion. I heard him blowing his nose like a trumpet afore ever I saw him. The noise were enough to bring that slag-heap down.'

Mildew waved her red flag towards another truck that stood beside a heap of slag.

'Is he here?' asked Robin.

From behind the slag-heap came a strange trumpeting noise. It *was* the sound of trumpeting but not the kind that trumpeters make when they puff out their cheeks and blow.

'There he goes again,' said Mildew. 'VERY second class! You wouldn't think he'd have had time to get back.'

Everybody had been so busy talking that nobody had noticed Worzel Gummidge's descent from the truck of coal-dust. Now he shambled towards them. His broom-stick arms were outstretched, and coal-dust drifted from his coat-sleeves. His shirt, usually the faded blue of a robin's egg, was streaked with coal-dust. His turnip face was black, and so were his bottle-straw boots.

Robin gazed at him enviously.

'What a sight he looks!' said Marlene.

'Worzel! Oh, Worzel, love!' cried Earthy.

'Shoo! Shoo!' shouted Mildew, waving her red flag.

Worzel Gummidge might have answered or he might have fallen into one of his ordinary sulks, but again and very suddenly the sound of trumpeting rose from behind the slag heap.

'There he goes again,' said Mildew Turmut. 'Very second class, he must be. Folks ought to learn to be quiet with their noses. I've a mind to scare him off o' the premises.'

She waved her red flag angrily, and took a few clattering steps towards the slag-heap.

'Don't talk so daft, and don't act so daft!' warned Gummidge. 'Stands to reason it's more like to scare you. There's no knowin' what slugs'll do once they're roused.'

'I've never seen a roused slug, Worzel, love,' put in little Earthy Mangold, tweaking her raspberry coloured veil aside, so that her face could be seen. It was a dear, kind, but not very pretty potatoish face.

'Then you've not seen this one lumping about on its four grey legs, and wavin' its two tails!' Gummidge told her. 'Bigger nor a cow it is, and its horns slipped down in front of its face.'

Earthy did not often argue with her husband, but she did so now.

'Slugs hasn't got no legs nor tails neither, Worzel. Maybe it's not a slug, or else it's a poor slug gone wrong.'

'It must be the elephant for the circus,' said Robin.

It *was* the elephant for the circus. As Robin stopped speaking, it came lumbering from behind the slag-heap. A length of chain dangled from its neck, and it was waving its trunk.

'It's a nelephant!' shouted Mildew. 'I've seen 'em afore. I've seen 'em in cattle-trucks.'

'There's no such word, and there's no such animal. Ooh aye! Stands to reason,' said Gummidge. 'Tails grow at the back – not out o' the middle o' faces.'

Robin tried to show off the knowledge of one glorious day spent at the Zoo. 'That isn't a tail: it's a trunk.'

'Trees keep their trunks to theirsels,' muttered Gummidge. 'They don't dangle 'em down in front o' gone-wrong slugs' faces.'

'Don't talk so iggerant, Worzel. There's more nor one sort o' trunk. There's railway trunks that passengers keeps their clothes in.' Mildew waved her flags at the elephant, who was plodding steadily towards her, and shouted 'Mind your backs!' Then, as the creature came closer, she added, very politely, 'Tickets, PLEASE.'

As elephants go, it was a small one, but seen so frighteningly close, it looked simply enormous.

Marlene dodged behind Earthy, and the little scarecrow spoke up bravely, 'It's a cow, that's what it is. It's a cow that's overgrown its poor strength and grown extra bits in the wrong places. Did ever you see anything so pitiful?'

The elephant trumpeted dolefully, as though in agreement. Then, waving its trunk towards Earthy, it snatched off her raspberry-pink veil, and waved it upwards.

Marlene shrieked, but Earthy, looking very odd indeed and tossing the sprouting potato leaves that made her hair, said kindly, 'It wants to cover its face, and no wonder it does, poor thing. Its mother did ought to be ashamed of herself.' Pity forced her to take two steps towards the animal.

But the elephant did not seem to mind about its face. It swirled the veil up beyond its head, dropped it on its shoulders, and then waved its trunk towards Worzel Gummidge.

'Look out!' shouted Robin, but he spoke too late, for the trunk curled round the scarecrow's body, and lifted him up, up, up, and then down, to sit – his broomstick legs straggled across the great back – just behind the pink veil.

Earthy shrieked, Robin shouted, Marlene burst into tears, while Mildew blew her whistle and waved her flags.

The elephant took not the slightest notice. Perhaps it was tired of the station yard. It padded away, its great knees wrinkling, out into the road. Children and scarecrows followed.

2 Sea-lions and Cod

The day was hot, the air was so still, and the elephant's footsteps were so regular that excitement faded.

'It can't be true,' thought Robin. 'No, it can't be true. I can't be following an elephant with Worzel Gummidge on his back. I must be dreaming. I'll wake up soon; then where shall I be?'

But the warmth and the definite hardness of the key in his pocket reminded him that he was not dreaming – that this was just a red-letter day.

'Worzel, love! Oh, Worzel, love!' murmured Earthy as green tears showered down her cheeks.

On and on ambled the elephant towards the outskirts of Scatterbrook village.

Suddenly the elephant stopped, ambled on to the grass that bordered the road, opened a gate by pushing it with its head, walked into a field, and came to a stop in front of a cattle-trough.

A few cows who were grazing in a far corner stopped their work and gazed at it.

'This water is not suitable for drinking purposes!' shouted Mildew importantly.

The elephant had not stopped to drink, but to wash.

It filled its trunk with water, and curled it round. First it sprayed one hindquarter and then the other.

'Don't let it drown my Worzel!' pleaded Earthy. 'Please don't let it drown my Worzel!'

The elephant dipped its trunk, and squirted some rather warm and rather muddy water, first over Robin, who liked it, and then over Marlene, who did not like it at all.

'Don't act so daft!' shouted Gummidge, from his place on the creature's back. 'Stands to reason you're not a hose-pipe, so there's no sense in boastin' and actin' like one!'

The elephant dipped its trunk again into the horse-trough, which was by now nearly empty. There was a thick squelchy noise.

'Come down, Worzel, love,' begged Earthy. 'Do please to jump down.'

Gummidge had twisted Earthy's raspberry net round his head over his hat and he scowled down at her.

'Don't talk so daft!' he said. 'Stands to reason I'm not a grasshopper. Stands to reason I'll not demean myself to jump. If what I'm sittin' on has the manners to sit, I'll step down dignified.'

Earthy twisted her twiggy fingers together. Green tears rained down her face as she looked at Mildew Turmut. 'Seein' as you're his only sister, maybe you'll know what to do.'

'There's only one way to make that nelephant lay down, and that's to keep it runnin' till it comes to a sit-still,' replied the railway scarecrow. 'We'd the same trouble once with a mad engine. They kept on drivin' it till it ran out o' puff.'

'Can you drive a nelephant, Mildew, love?' asked Earthy.

'If I can scare trains, I can drive elephants,' said Mildew.

She ducked her head, caught up her whistle in her mouth, and waved her red flag in the elephant's face. Slowly, the creature began to lumber across the field. Mildew shambled after it, and Earthy followed, uttering little bird-like cries.

Just as Robin was going to join the scarecrows, Marlene stopped wringing drops of muddy water from the hem of her skirt.

'Listen!' she said.

From the main street of Scatterbrook village, there sounded shrill blasts from another whistle.

'The fish!' cried Marlene. 'Come on quick, or I'll cop it.'

The edge of her dripping frock whipped against her knees as she ran. Robin followed her. He didn't know why except that she would 'cop it' unless he did.

Now, a visiting fishmonger drove his van into Scatterbrook each Saturday and Wednesday morning. When he pulled up his van in the main street, he shrilled on his whistle to warn people he was there.

The fishmonger's van was drawn up opposite to the Post Office. By the time Robin and Marlene reached it, there was a crowd of people. Nearly everyone was holding a plate.

Mr Hale, the fishmonger, had stopped blowing his whistle, and was talking rather loudly. 'Now then, ladies, I've a fine lot of fish this morning – fresh herring, fresh mackerel, good fillets of cod and hake, skate and whiting, kippers. Take your choice.'

Mrs Kibbins, the owner of what was now Earthy's veil, pushed a plate towards Mr Hale, and asked, 'Have you any nice cod's roe this morning?'

'Any nice cod roe,' repeated Mr Hale. 'I'll have a look-see.'

Marlene was whispering to Robin, 'My Mum's gone to Dimden market. She said I was to take a plate and buy a nice bit of cod fillet. There's no time to get a plate now. Have you any paper in your pocket?'

Robin had not, and he said so.

'Your hankie would do: it's bigger than mine,' suggested Marlene.

More people crowded round the back of the van. 'Stand back, ladies, IF you please, and give me a chance to open the van doors,' said Mr Hale.

And now, as people shuffled backwards, clattering plates, muttering, and treading on one another's toes, strange sounds came from the inside of the van. They were shriller and more plaintive than roars or bellowings. They were richer and deeper and more musical than the mooing of Bessie, the one-horned cow.

'Sounds like you've a wild animal in there,' said Mrs Kibbins. Robin thought the same thing, and knuckled his freckled forehead as he tried to remember where he had heard those particular noises before. They were not the sounds of the countryside: they belonged to London, and to one particular hot afternoon when the reek of lions and tigers had mingled with the smell of raw meat, when an elephant had snatched a bun from his fingers, a bear had caught another one, and he had watched a keeper flinging herrings to – yes – to sea-lions.

Mr Hale was wrenching at the handles of the van doors which had jammed. At last he wrenched them open, and the shoppers surged forward. From their place at the back of the crowd, the children listened to remarks and exclamations that were not usually heard in Scatterbrook's peaceful street.

'Cruel, I call it, selling live fish!'

'Look at the ugly great things!'

'Look at their flippers!'

'Great lolloping, flabby, floppy things! What are they?'

Robin, who had pushed his way to the front, and was peering into the van, answered the last question.

'They're sea-lions!' he said, and wished he had not spoken, for Mr Hale slammed the doors shut, and turned on him.

'Sea-lions they are,' he agreed, 'and seeing you know so much, p'raps you'll tell me where they've come from?'

'Dunno,' said Robin. 'But they're going to the circus.'

'They are, are they? Then they'll go to it by the police station,' snapped Mr Hale. 'Those savage things have eaten up half my stock, and spoiled the rest.' He stepped back on to a piece of rock salmon, fallen from the van. Marlene scooped it up, and snatched Robin's handkerchief from his pocket as a wrapping. Then she picked up a couple of herrings and a half-eaten whiting.

Now there is no police station in Scatterbrook, but there is a policeman, and he lodges in a house quite near to Finch Cottage.

Mr Hale climbed into the driving seat, honked his horn to clear the road in front of him, and drove away. Soon the annoyed voices of the sea-lions were heard no more. People carried their empty plates back into their cottages. Robin and Marlene were left alone. There was nothing except some fish scales and a few battered shrimps lying in the dust to show that anything unusual had happened.

'We'd better go back and tell that Fat Lady what's happened,' said Marlene. 'She might like to buy some fish.'

'She put us in charge of the sea-lions,' said Robin. 'We'd better go after them.'

As he sprinted along the road, with Marlene beside him, he wondered how he could look after sea-lions, even if he could rescue them from the van. He supposed they ought to live in a pond. How much food should they have? Could he and Marlene fish enough minnows from the Scatterbrook stream?

'Sea-lions and elephants! Anything could happen on a day like this,' thought Robin as he jogged along. 'Sea-lions and elephants.' His footsteps beat out the rhythm of the words in his head.

Yet, though he felt that anything could happen, he had not expected anything so lucky as that Mr Hale should have had a puncture just outside Finch Cottage. The jack under the wheel told the story. Mr Hale was not there: he had gone to borrow a wrench from the policeman, and to tell his own sad tale.

'The wash-house!' cried Robin. 'That's the place for them! I'll unlock the door. You undo the van and dangle the fish at them.'

Marlene, who had not, and naturally, followed his thought, gasped and gaped at him.

'Hurry!' yelled Robin, and hurried himself.

The key slid into the lock, clicked, and then the door of Finch Cottage stood invitingly open – ready to welcome sea-lions. Robin dashed back down the garden path, snatched Marlene's handkerchief full of fish, wrenched open the van doors, and said, 'Come along out. Good dogs! Good dogs!' He could not speak sea-lion language, but the creatures understood. They came lolloping down from the van, stretching out their whiskered noses towards the fishy handkerchief.

'Shut the van doors!' yelled Robin, and Marlene shut them, as the creatures, looking as though they were dressed in well-fitting black oil-skins, lumbered swiftly up the flagged path between the lavender borders and over the threshold. In another minute Marlene had followed, and the door of Finch Cottage was locked from the inside.

Luckily the sea-lions had dined so well from Mr Hale's cod, whiting, herrings, hake, rock-salmon, shrimps and mackerel that they were not at all hungry. Otherwise they might have been snappy.

However, they *were* thirsty. Perhaps they smelled water. Most obligingly, they followed Robin into the wash-house. There, while Marlene looked on, they looked up while he put the stopper into the sink and turned the taps.

'You'll never get them up there,' said Marlene.

'I'm going to flood the floor!' said Robin daringly.

Now there was a backless kitchen chair in the wash-house. One of the sea-lions jumped on to it, and there stayed, stretching its thick neck and waving it hopefully from side to side. Robin, who had been to some big circuses in London, guessed at once what it wanted. Luckily, what it wanted was close at hand – there was a bright yellow ball on a ledge behind the sink. He tossed it towards the sea-lion, who caught it on its nose and began to juggle with it. Presently it bounded off, and the other creature caught it. They did their best to give a good performance, but perhaps the ball was not the right size or made of the right sort of stuff. Soon it fell with a splash into the water that was overflowing the sink, and creeping towards Marlene.

'I'm not going to stay here and be half drowned!' she said, and opened the wash-house door. Robin splashed after her, and slammed the door behind him.

The sea-lions could stay where they were. It was time to see what was happening to Worzel Gummidge and Mildew Turmut AND the elephant.

He remembered his promise to Aunt Ruby.

'I've got to open the windows,' he said, and charged upstairs. Marlene followed.

As soon as the windows in the little front bedroom that was to be Robin's own were opened, the children heard voices. One was loud and angry: the other was gruff and obstinate.

Mr Hale was talking to the policeman.

'You can see for yourself!' he said, and flung the doors of the van wide open.

The policeman whisked his note-book from his pocket, and stepped forward cautiously. 'Well?' he said, 'what's all the bother about?'

'Well!' exclaimed Mr Hale. 'Well, I'll be jiggered! But they *were* there.'

'Who was?' asked the policeman.

'Sea-lions, I told you. I shut them in tight: they couldn't have got out by themselves.'

'Maybe they've slipped through the cracks in the floorboards,' suggested the policeman helpfully, and he knelt down to peer under the van.

'*Sea-lions* slipped through the cracks in the floorboards,' shouted Mr Hale. 'They was nearly as big as you are. You ought to have seen them. If you've ever seen sea-lions you'd know.'

The policeman helped Mr Hale to put on his spare wheel. Then they continued to argue. The policeman straightened his helmet, and said, 'The police can't be responsible for what's put in or taken out of unattended vans. Did you leave your van unattended?'

'Only for a few minutes or so,' admitted Mr Hale.

Out came the policeman's note-book again. 'Where did you leave it?'

'At the back door of Railway Cottage about nine o'clock

time. I couldn't make anyone hear so I went round to the front door that opened on to the platform.'

The policeman's lips moved as he wrote. Then he looked up, and asked, 'Did you see anyone?'

'Not for a bit, I hammered and hammered. Then I went to the ticket-office to find Bert. We may have had a bit of a chat, not for more than a minute or two.'

The policeman looked up warningly.

'Well, not above ten minutes. Bert told me Mrs Bolton had gone by train.'

'Unattended van,' remarked the policeman. 'Did you look to see if the sea-lions were inside before you drove off?'

'Would anyone look for sea-lions in their vans?' asked Mr Hale angrily.

The policeman considered his answer. 'It's always best to take precautions,' he said. Then he closed his note-book and walked towards the cottage gate.

'It's lucky you happened to mention Mrs Bolton. She asked me to look round Finch Cottage every so often in case the boy forgot.'

For a moment Robin felt indignant, as most of us do when we find we're not expected to do something good that we have done. Then he felt triumphant as he remembered that he had locked the door from inside.

'You can wait a minute, and then I'll come with you,' shouted the policeman. 'Mrs Bolton gave me the spare key!'

Robin felt in his pocket. Yes, his own key was there. If only he had left it in the lock the policeman would not have been able to open the door! He dragged Marlene back from the window and looked wildly round the empty room.

Down below, the sea-lions raised their voices in a musical bawling.

Suddenly Robin noticed the big white-painted cupboard that took up the whole of one wall. Its key was in the lock. This time he would be careful.

'Quick!' he said. 'We'll have to hide in there.'

'I don't like dark cupboards,' whimpered Marlene, standing very firmly in the middle of the room, 'you never know what's inside them.'

That was very true, as she discovered when, having decided that she liked policemen even less than 'things' in dark cupboards, she let Robin drag her behind the doors. He had removed the key, and was now fumbling to fit it into the lock. Luckily there were some large ventilation holes high up in the door, so the cupboard was not quite dark.

'You're treadin' on my face!' moaned Hannah Harrow, the invalid scarecrow, and Marlene, feeling something soft beneath her foot, let out a shriek.

Luckily, the noise of the sea-lions below was louder than any child's voice.

Robin turned the key and pulled it out of the lock. By the light that streamed through the keyhole, he and Marlene could just make out the sad ungainly form of Hannah Harrow sprawled at the bottom of the cupboard.

'My face is bad enough without bein' trod on,' she whimpered.

That was quite true, though it was not light enough to see the scarecrow's tarred boot-lace hair or her melancholy features. Her face was stuffed, and so were her legs – one much more tightly than the other. She wore a fish-basket hat, the sacking skirt that is the uniform of so many lady scarecrows, and a shawl made from old muslin curtains. The children knew this, though they could not see very clearly.

'What arc you doing here?' asked Robin.

'I were scarin' moths until the moths started scarin' me,' whined Hannah. 'It were Mr Gummidge thought about it first, "All you're fit for's to scare moths", he said, and Upsidaisy – her that's so eddicated – happened to remark as how the littlest moths lived indoors off of human woollen clothes. I don't wear woollens meself – not outside. I'd forgot me bad heart.'

'Norma's aunty has a bad heart, too,' said Marlene.

'Have the moth got at it?' Hannah, too interested in her own ailments, did not wait for an answer. 'She can't be so bad as me if the moth haven't got at it. My heart's made out o' a bit o' red felt left over from when Miss Dollit took to toy-makin'.' She flapped one of her hooky hands across her chest, and a cloud of moths flew up, and flitted round the cupboard. They were enchanted into gold, as they flew across the shaft of light, streaming from the keyhole.

'The big mothery's in the corner,' said Hannah.

Robin, exploring, found an old rag rug that, somehow and strangely, had been left behind by his Aunt Ruby when she moved from Finch Cottage. He stirred it with his foot, and more clouds of moths flew out.

'First it was mice and then it's moths,' groaned Hannah. 'I don't know which is worser. Mice nibbled holes in my legs so the sawdust stuffin' ran out, and now the moths is eatin' their dinners off of my poor heart.'

'Shut up!' said Robin suddenly.

Heavy footsteps were coming up the stairs – two lots of footsteps, and he guessed that Mr Hale was following the policeman up into the bedroom.

Then the footsteps came to a stop.

Mr Hale spoke – 'Nothing here,' he said.

'Doesn't look like it,' agreed the policeman. 'Best see if there's anything in this cupboard.'

Doors rattled but they held. Robin, trying to block the key-hole with his body, stepped on Hannah's face, and the sick scarecrow gave a series of little whimpering squeaks.

'Mice by the sound,' remarked the policeman.

Mr Hale said he was not interested in mice. He was interested in discovering who had put sea-lions into his van, and who was going to pay for the fish they had eaten. 'And now you've seen them for yourself,' he added. 'Now you've seen them for yourself, perhaps you'll tell *me* if they could have slipped through the hole in the van floor?'

'Best thing we can do is to get them back into the van, and drive them to the circus.' Perhaps the policeman thought it better not to answer Mr Hale's last question. 'There was a bit of sheep-netting hanging on the fence: we can use that.'

From down below the voices of the sea-lions were raised, as though in protest.

3 The Elephant Trainer

A long, it seemed a very long, time afterwards, Robin opened the cupboard door, and tiptoed out into the room. Marlene followed him, and Hannah, cobwebs entangled in her tarred boot-lace hair, moths fluttering above her red felt heart, crawled out after them.

The children hurried to the window and looked out. The van had gone. Sloshy trails of water on the flagstoned path showed that the sea-lions had gone with it. A few broken branches told that the sheep-netting had been dragged from the hedge.

'Come on!' said Robin impatiently, and dashed downstairs, followed by Marlene.

Mr Hale or the policeman had turned off the taps above the sink, but the place was awash with water.

With a little thud, Hannah Harrow landed at the foot of the stairs, down which she had, somehow, managed to flop.

She crawled towards them, and as she did this, the children noticed that she left an almost dry trail behind her. The fact was that her sawdust stuffing was very dry, and mopped up the water as readily as a sponge.

As she crawled into the wash-house, she spoke almost cheerfully. 'This'll drown the moths, and give 'em shocking bad colds in the head. It'll give 'em screwmatics besides. Maybe drowned moths with colds in the heads and screwmatics won't have the heart to keep on chewin' my heart away.'

It was wonderful to see how much water the invalid scarecrow took up. By the time she had finished her journeyings round the wash-house, the floor was almost dry, though rather streaky, and Hannah's legs and arms and body were swollen to about three times their usual size. A few dishevelled cloth-moths clung to her boot-lace hair.

'I've got the fatness and dampness!' she moaned. 'Very distressin' illness fatness and dampness is. One's bad enough without t'other.'

The children dragged her water-logged body out through the back door, and laid it to dry on a sunny rubbish heap. When Robin had locked the front door and pocketed the key, he and Marlene hurried away in seach of Worzel Gummidge and the elephant.

The Fat Lady was at the door of her tent, and she was talking to a man who wore a yellow waistcoat, and had a red handkerchief tied round his neck. Robin guessed that he was Mr Biltong, the owner of the circus.

'It's no use asking *me*,' he was saying. 'It's no use asking me how the sea-lions got into the fish van. They were in their cage when I went off, and when I came back the door was open.'

'When you went off *where*, I'd like to know?' The Fat Lady's chins wobbled impatiently.

'I had to find a farmer, hadn't I, to see if I could buy some hay for fodder?'

'*And* you had to let the sea-lions get out, *and* leave me to try to laugh it off with a policeman, who didn't know if he was going or coming, and a fishmonger who wanted to be paid for a ton or more of fish. AND you had to leave me to receive the elephant *and* the elephant trainer.'

The children, who had crept closer to listen, and who knew by instinct that the two grown-up people (one *very* grown-up indeed, and grown in many directions) were too busy to bother about *them*, noticed that Mr Biltong looked puzzled.

'Nor,' continued the Fat Lady, having drawn breath, 'nor did you think of happening to mention that a trainer was coming with the elephant. Not that that's a bad thing, though I can scarcely understand a word of what he's talking about. You can't expect these foreign trainers to talk the same as we do.'

Robin nudged Marlene. Like Mr Biltong, he thought it wisest not to speak. So the elephant and Worzel Gummidge had arrived at the circus!

'Nor you didn't happen to mention the others neither. Oh no!'

'What others?' Mr Biltong spoke at last, and in a squeaky nervous voice.

'What others indeed? You must have engaged them or they wouldn't be here. One's gate-keeper, and she talks queerly, too. I couldn't make out most of it, but she kept on shouting "Tickets, please". She wanted to make me understand she knew her job, I suppose. One thing is, she looked fierce enough to keep out the lads that say they're under twelve and half price, when you can see they're growing out of their fathers' trousers. I can't make the other one out at all.'

'What other one?' asked Mr Biltong unwisely.

'You may well ask what other one! The one that says she's an animal comforter and the trainer's wife. What's she supposed to do?'

Mr Biltong clutched his head.

'You've forgotten, I suppose, same as you've forgotten to shut the sea-lion's cage. How many more are coming that I don't know about?'

Mr Biltong swallowed nervously, and then he changed the subject.

'You leave it to me, ducks. You'll take too much out of yourself if you go on like that.'

Suddenly, perhaps she liked being addressed as 'ducks', the fat woman smiled. 'You're right there, Biltong, I've got to look after my figure. There's no sense putting it on if I fret it off.' She stretched out her arms and yawned mightily. 'I'll have another snack, and see if I can't sleep it on.'

The children, anxious that she should have her rest before she noticed them, dodged behind her tent. From there they heard her asking another question, 'Did you get the hay from the farmer?'

'He wasn't in.'

'Then you'd better see to it now while I have forty winks or so. The elephant'll be all right with the trainer. The sea-lions are in the spare cages.'

The canvas at the back of the tent billowed and bulged. There was a creaking sound which told the children that the Fat Lady was settling down on her bed. She spoke again, in a sleepy voice, 'When you come back, you can give the merry-go-round a trial run. Better do it tonight with the lights on.' Her words slurred into a yawn.

The children stood still and watched Mr Biltong scurrying away from the recreation ground.

At last they were alone with a circus. They heard in the distance the trumpeting of the elephant. Presently, the snores of the Fat Lady mingled with the sound.

A flutter of pink showed above and behind the merry-go-round. They knew that it must be Worzel Gummidge's turban – once Earthy Mangold's raspberry-netting veil.

'Come on!' said Robin, and they pelted across the grass, skipping over a litter of tent-poles and guy ropes.

The elephant had picked up a tent-peg in its trunk, and was waving it idly to and fro.

'Mind your backs!' shouted Mildew Turmut importantly. 'Children under twelve half-price.'

Earthy was looking up at Worzel Gummidge, who was a-straddle still on the elephant's back.

'Oh, Worzel, love, come down, do. You look like what a mouse might feel sittin' on top of a mole-hill when the mole-hill was bein' throwed up – all wobbly and bumpy.'

'I could scare crows a lot better from here,' answered Gummidge. 'Stands to reason, I could scare high-flyin' crows and aeryoplanes.' He stretched out his broomstick arms as he boasted, and the breeze stirred his coat-sleeves.

Earthy looked round and noticed the children. As is the way of scarecrows she began to talk as though they had not been parted for more than a minute or two.

'It's very complicate,' she said. 'That lady-human with the lot o' dewlaps—'

'Dewlaps?' interrupted Robin, and Marlene, who had spent all her ten years in the country, explained, 'Dewlaps are what cows have instead of chins. Bessie has one.'

'This human has a lot,' continued Earthy, and a shower of green tears ran down her cheeks. 'She wants Mildew to take the tickets, and Mr Gummidge to train the elephant, but she doesn't know what an animal comforter is. Very iggerant she must be. Asides, it's not only animals I comforts – it's birds and insecks and fish and snails and all sorts. Fish is most complicate acos they're so skiddy. Snails is complicate, too: you casn't hear 'em sobbin' when they tucks 'emsels back in their houses.'

Mildew, who had been waving her green flag sulkily, cried that as she knew all about trains she ought to *train* the elephant. She began to talk to the creature in rapid *Railway* – 'Big trunks must go in the luggage compartment, NOT on the rack. Racks are for light articles only. No smoking! Ladies only! Reserved! All change! All change! All change!'

The elephant tossed the tent-peg away, stretched out its trunk towards Mildew, seized her red flag and waved it high in the air.

Worzel Gummidge looked down at his indignant sister.

'Maybe that'll learn you,' he said. 'Ooh aye! Maybe that'll learn you as the elephant don't fancy bein' trained by you.'

Robin asked a question, 'Did *you* put the sea-lions into the fishmonger's van when he left it by the station yard this morning?'

'Ooh aye! Leastways, I put some planks alongside so's they could slither up.'

Just then the elephant decided to sit down. It dropped its hindquarters and doubled its knees suddenly enough to jerk the scarecrow from its back. Then, settling itself more comfortably, it rested part of its enormous bulk on the edge of his coat. There, back to back, sat Worzel Gummidge and the elephant.

Marlene shrieked, Earthy Mangold hopped from foot to foot, Mildew Turmut blew her whistle, and Robin wondered what to do.

'He'll have to take his coat off,' said Marlene.

'Very second class cheap excursion that'd be.'

The edge of the red flag that was being waved by the elephant had flipped the whistle out of Mildew's mouth.

'He's not easy-joined enough to get out of a sat-on coat,' sobbed Earthy.

Worzel Gummidge, his pink turban resting against the elephant's flank, his face black and sulky-looking, said, 'I told it to sit and it sat. When we've finishing sittin', I'll tell it to get up. This nelephant does all I says. I told it to sit!'

'Oh, Worzel, LOVE, you never—' began Earthy.

Very, very foolishly indeed, Marlene interrupted – 'You great big story! I was watching all the time.'

A few trickles of coal-dust ran down Worzel Gummidge's turnip cheeks, as he settled his face into a sulky expression.

'You've drove me to it,' he said. 'Me and the elephant's goin' to have a real good sulk. Seein' *it's* so big, the sulk'll be a bigger one nor usual.'

As though in agreement, the elephant twitched an ear and closed its eyes.

From past experience (not with elephants but with scarecrows) Robin knew there was nothing to be done.

Mildew's whistle was in her mouth again, and she blew a series of long blasts.

A clown stepped down from a near-by caravan. At least

Robin supposed he was a clown because he was wearing white cotton trousers with frills round the ankles. His top half was dressed ordinarily in an open-necked shirt and a grey pullover. His right cheek was as swollen as though he had pouched an orange in it.

'You don't want to whistle like that,' he said, 'you'll wake old Ma Biltong.'

He glanced at the curious group but did not seem surprised at their oddness.

'You'll be the new turns,' he remarked. 'My name's Pick-me-up, the world-famous doctor, but it's spelt PERKINS.'

Worzel Gummidge continued to sulk and the elephant to sleep. Mildew Turmut blew a shrill defiant blast from her whistle, and Earthy Mangold hopped forward.

'If your name's Pick-me-up, please to pick me up me husbin' from unner the nelephant.'

The doctor (he did not look like the doctor who visited Robin in London, or like Dr Moon of Scatterbrook) shook his head.

'The last elephant we had went on like that. I remember the day he went to sleep on poor old Ali's foot in the middle of a performance. There was Ali screaming, and there was the crowd shouting at me to cure him with a bottle of my famous cure-all. Ma Biltong's the only one who can shift elephants when they're not in the mood to budge, but it's as much as my place is worth to wake her in the afternoon.'

He seemed to notice the children for the first time, and asked, 'Have you two anything to do with the circus?'

'Sort of,' Robin spoke cautiously, and Marlene added, 'We've to look after the sea-lions.'

'That's all right then.' Pick-me-up looked relieved. 'I'm not supposed to be seen out with this face. It's stopped aching all that much but the swelling won't go down. I'd not be much of an advertisement for *cure-all* with a face like this. Have you seen old Biltong yet?'

Robin nodded.

'Nice enough little fellow, but he don't know if he's going or coming. Ma Biltong's the one, but she's not the time to see to everything on account of having to sleep it on, and spending so long about it. I lend a hand all round. Come to me if you want anything.'

Worzel Gummidge opened his eyes and glared at him. He stretched up a broomstick arm and thumped the elephant.

'Gee up!' he shouted.

Now, whether the elephant had rested for long enough, or whether there was a strange understanding between it and Worzel Gummidge is a thing that may never be known. Anyway, it lumbered to its feet, stretched out its trunk, picked up the scarecrow, set him on his back, and reached down for Mildew's flag before turning to lumber across the recreation ground in the direction of the Fat Lady's tent.

'I'll say that fellow can train elephants!' said Pick-me-up admiringly.

He followed: and Mildew and Earthy came after him.

Marlene and the children hesitated because they saw that Mr Hale's van was pulled up by the Fat Lady's tent.

Mr Hale had had a very tiresome day. It had been bad enough to find sea-lions in his van, to lose his trade, and to waste his morning. It had been worse to find the Fat Lady so unhelpful. She had yawned in his face, and said, 'If you've any complaints, you can make them to Biltong, and he's not here. I mustn't be worried: it's bad for my figure. AND I'll not have sea-lions gallivanting about my tent when I'm trying to get a bit of sleep.'

A boy who helped to work the merry-go-round had helped to settle the creatures into a spare cage, and because there was nothing else to be done, Mr Hale had driven away.

There were several children in the village street. One of them shouted, 'Got any sea-lion steak this afternoon?'

Another one yelled, 'I'll have some filleted flipper!'

'You can drop me at my cottage,' said the policeman,

cross because the bottoms of his trouser-legs were heavy with the water from the wash-house floor. 'I've got to bike to Dimden this afternoon to sell tickets for the Police Concert. I've done enough wild-goose chasing for one afternoon.'

'Sea-*lion* chasing, you mean,' corrected Mr Hale rather nastily. 'If you won't help, I shall have to get the sergeant from Dimden.'

'We'll find the fellow who did it all in good time,' boasted the policeman.

But Mr Hale, having driven away from the policeman's cottage, decided he would find out for himself, and in better than good time.

'Criminals always go back to the scene of the crime,' he thought. 'There may be someone lurking about Finch Cottage.'

He stopped his van, opened the doors so that fresh air could blow away the smell of fish and sea-lions, and opened the little gate. First he peered through the sitting-room window, then he pressed against a water-butt and looked in at the kitchen. Both rooms were empty, and there was nothing in the scullery except a coloured ball and the backless chair.

A ladder was lying in the little patch of garden at the side of the cottage. With its help, he would be able to look in through the upstairs windows.

'There's nothing like being thorough,' he thought, as he leaned the ladder against the wall.

Now, Mr Hale, who disliked fish-scales on his trousers, always wore a long blue apron when he was out on his rounds. Because he thought it looked dignified, he wore a black bowler hat. Neither aprons nor bowler-hats make ladder climbing easier. He kept treading on the apron as he went up, and he kept catching his bowler hat on the low thatch of the roof as he looked in through the windows.

By this time Hannah Harrow was a great deal drier than she had been. She had crawled off the rubbish heap, had managed to stand upright, and was making her way to the front gate where she met Upsidaisy, the educated scarecrow, who worked on the school allotments.

On fine Saturdays Upsidaisy often took a holiday, or did odd scaring jobs in other gardens and allotments, for she was a sociable little creature. Besides, by going from place to place, she added to the knowledge of geography which she had learned from listening under the school windows.

Many a shrunken sock, missed from a Scatterbrook clothes line, had been taken by Upsidaisy, who trundled about on her three milking-stool legs.

'My!' said Upsidaisy. 'My! You've put on a lot of weight, Hannah Harrow. Have you been give some new stuffin'?'

'I've been give the dampness and the heaviness!' moaned the invalid scarecrow. 'The moths have been at me heart somethink cruel. It's a very unhealthy place this is. Help me away, Upsidaisy.'

The three-legged scarecrow stretched out her little gloved hand and patted Hannah. The glove was stuffed with paper, and rustled as cheerfully and mysteriously as a well-filled Christmas stocking.

'Where did you think o' goin'?' she asked.

'Anywhere so long as its beyond moth-flight.'

'Moths flies miles and miles when they're in lovin' moods,' said Upsidaisy, anxious as usual to show off her knowledge. 'A genelman moth'll fly miles an' miles an' miles an' MILES to reach a lady moth when he loves her.'

'The moths as ate me poor heart wasn't genelmen moths,' answered Hannah. 'Very ungenelmanly it is to chew a lady's heart.'

'If they was lady moths, and there's any of 'em left, then the genelmen moths'll fly miles and miles an' miles an' miles to reach 'em,' said Upsidaisy. 'You're not a fast walker, Hannah Harrow, nor am I, on account o' havin' to trundle. Maybe we'd better drive.'

She waved a gloved hand towards the opened doors of Mr Hale's van.

Somehow or other, the two scarecrows managed to clamber inside. The fishmonger did not see them because, by this time, he was peeping in at a back bedroom window.

'Where'll we be drivin' *to*?' asked Hannah Harrow, leaning her head, with its straggling boot-lace hair, against the side of the van, and sagging into a sitting position.

Upsidaisy trundled into a corner behind the door. It was impossible for her to sit because her three legs were so difficult to manage. Her velveteen coat reached nearly to the tops of her three different coloured socks. Her sailor hat was pushed to the back of her head. She looked a little worried because she hated not knowing the answer to the question.

'Where'll we be drivin' *to*?' repeated Hannah.

'That depends how far we goes.' Upsidaisy tried to remember past geography lessons. 'Seein' the world's round like a norange, if we keeps on drivin' far enough we'll come back where we started from.'

'I don't want to come back where we started from!' screamed Hannah. 'I wants to go away from where the genelman moths is comin' from.'

'It won't make no differ,' Upsidaisy told her. 'The world keeps on goin' round and round the sun. That's jography. If we stays where we are we comes back to the same place.'

'Now you've give me the dizzies!' wailed Hannah Harrow.

Just then the van darkened. Mr Hale, having finished peeping into windows, had slammed the doors without troubling to look inside them. As he drove away, Upsidaisy continued her 'jography' lesson.

'There's a belt goes round the middle o' the world, and it's called the equator.'

'I'd a belt once that went round the middle o' my stummick. It were made from a bit o' wire, but the rust got at it. I've been a cruel sufferer from rust,' moaned Hannah.

There was silence for a little, and then she spoke again.

'I hope we're not drivin' to meet any o' these genelmen moths.'

Presently, and for the second time that day, Mr Hale stopped his van outside the Fat Lady's tent.

It was then that Marlene and Robin saw it, but, though they longed to know what would happen next, Robin did not want to be questioned about the sea-lions' adventure in the wash-house at Finch Cottage.

'Come on,' he said, and pulled Marlene behind an empty caravan. From there they watched. It was like looking in at a television play with the sound turned off.

Worzel Gummidge rode the elephant proudly towards the entrance to the tent. Out came the Fat Lady. Down from his van jumped Mr Hale, while Mildew waved her green flag, and the elephant brandished the red one high above its head. Earthy looked from one to another, and everyone, except the elephant, seemed to be talking at the same time. Pick-me-up spoke for longer than any of them.

Presently the elephant dropped the red flag (which was pounced on by Mildew Turmut) and lowered its trunk. Perhaps it could smell the fishiness of Mr Hale's van, or perhaps it was simply inquisitive. The soft end of its trunk came to rest on the door handles, and stayed there.

Pick-me-up went on talking, and it was clear that whatever he said was making the fishmonger very angry indeed.

Mr Hale looked furiously at the Fat Lady, and even more furiously at Pick-me-up. Then he jumped into the driving seat, started up the car, and drove away. As he did this the elephant twisted the tip of its trunk. The doors of the van flew open. Out toppled Upsidaisy and Hannah Harrow!

Marlene and Robin continued to look on; and now everything seemed as natural as a dream. Upsidaisy trundled cheerfully towards the Fat Lady. Earthy stretched out twiggy fingers to Hannah. By way of a change, the elephant snatched the green flag from the hand of the railway scarecrow.

Once again everyone (except the elephant) began to talk; and this time everyone seemed happy.

A great deal of attention was paid to Hannah Harrow, and she made the very most of it. She sagged and she flopped: she beat her heart until two moths flew out and drifted towards the children.

Upsidaisy trundled round on her milking-stool legs.

At last the Fat Lady yawned three times, and then backed into her tent. Pick-me-up hurried towards his own caravan, and Worzel Gummidge, still riding the elephant, led a procession of scarecrows to where the children were standing.

Earthy Mangold was the first to speak.

'We've been took on. We're Circus Acts now.'

'Ooh aye!' Worzel Gummidge looked proudly down, 'I'm a nelephant scarer now.'

'They said my three legs was worth a fortune!' squeaked Upsidaisy. 'They've never had a three-legs in the circus afore.'

'I've to cure all the sick people o' their ailments!' squealed Hannah Harrow. 'That nelephant's got a very unhealthy lookin' nose. Wait till it gets a bad cold and starts givin' out infections. I'll only cure those as has nelephant colds if they're perlite to me.'

The elephant twitched its trunk towards her in an offended sort of way, and Gummidge shouted, 'You're very unhealthy-lookin' yoursel, Hannah Harrow. That's why they've chose you to be doctor. You've to stand and shout – "Look at me, and take warnin'. Look at me, and drink CUTALL'S CURE-ALL afore this happens to YOU!" Ooh aye! I heard what they telled you to shout.'

Mildew Turmut blew her whistle and waved her red flag as though to give warning that a quarrel was about to begin, but Hannah only simpered.

There was no doubt that she had a plan. She was up to *something.*

From the tower below Scatterbrook's church steeple the clock chimed solemnly five times, and Marlene gave an unhappy little squeak.

'Mum'll be back from market. I should have been back to say I couldn't get that fish from Mr Hale. There'll be a carry-on, and no mistake.'

'Come back this evening, love,' said Earthy Mangold. 'Circus doesn't start till Monday, but all of us's have to have a bit o' practice.'

As Marlene, first fiddling with her hair ribbon, and then tugging at her socks, scudded across the recreation ground, Robin decided that girls were very queer. Fancy thinking about fish at a moment when the whole world had turned to magic! Fancy bothering about anything else!

Then, as so often happens when we think we are superior to other people, things became dull quite suddenly.

The elephant, still ridden by Gummidge, lumbered away. Earthy became interested in a grasshopper. Upsidaisy trundled about rather aimlessly. Hannah recited a long list of illnesses, and Mildew Turmut practised a mixture of railway and circus language – '*Sea-lions and elephants first-class-smoking-reserved. Special excursions by merry-go-round. Cheap-return day-trips by swing-boat. To stop the circus, pull the elephant's trunk. Penalty for improper use five pounds. This rack is for light articles only, and not for Fat Ladies.*'

Nobody seemed to be in the very least interested in Robin, so he wandered away.

4 An Evening at the Circus

Marlene's mother was tired and rather cross. She had had a long day at Dimden market, and had been looking forward to an easily cooked supper of fish and chips.

'I never knew such a girl for thinking up excuses,' she said. 'If you'd told me some of those cats from the farm had helped themselves from Mr Hale's van, I might have believed you. Whoever heard of sea-lions in Scatterbrook? No, you can't go to the circus. Anyway, it doesn't start till Monday.'

So, after a supper of bread and cheese, and a cup of dreary cocoa, made with water because the cat had overturned the milk-bottle, Marlene went up to the loft where she kept her collections of dustbin loot, broken toys that were waiting to be mended, lengths of string, pictures cut from newspapers, and all the other things that might one day be valuable. She found a tangle of fuse wire. Then, though it was rather painful, she began to tug out hairs from her own head. She might as well practise weaving the rings which she hoped might make her fortune. Perhaps human hairs were as lucky as elephant hairs. 'But I'm not a very lucky girl,' thought Marlene, as she tangled hairs and fuse wires into a fuzzy flimsy ring, 'not this evening, anyway!'

That was why Robin, having had supper with his Uncle Dick, was able to go alone to the circus.

Mr Bolton was a most convenient uncle because so long as a boy kept fairly quiet, and did not bother *him*, he did not bother the boy. Possibly he understood that the time when bacon is frizzling in a frying-pan and filling a kitchen with delicious scent is not the time for hair-brushing and knee-scrubbing and the care of fingernails. Nor did he bother about things being eaten in the right order. There was no bread-and-butter-before-cake-nonsense about Uncle Dick, and there were no warnings about the sort of food that should not be eaten in the evenings for fear of nightmares.

As Robin had explained so often to his Aunt Ruby, he rather *liked* nightmares. They might be frightening at the time, but he always woke up before anything had happened. In dreams, the most peculiar things happened quite naturally, almost as naturally as they happened in the daytime when scarecrows were about.

Robin, munching a sandwich made of thick slabs of cheese with hunks of tinned pineapple between them, hoped he would have an exciting dream that night.

'I shan't be back till five o'clock time,' announced Uncle Dick, who worked on the railway lines.

The clock on the chimney piece struck seven times, and Robin looked puzzled.

'I mean five o'clock in the morning.' Uncle Dick looked with interest at Robin's sandwich, and began to make one for himself. 'One of our chap's been taken to hospital, and I said I'd work his shift for him. I'll have a bit of a lay down when I've finished supper, and I'll start off again at ten. I won't shout out in case you're asleep. I'll leave the door unlocked – there's no sense in knocking you up at five.'

That was all. There was no telling Robin to be sure to be in bed by nine o'clock, no ordering him to scrub his knees in the bath, no worrying about the kitchen fire, no reminder to put out his clean clothes overnight because tomorrow was Sunday.

Uncle Dick finished his sandwich and stood up.

'I'll have a long lay-in when I come back in the morning,' he said. 'You do what you like.'

Perhaps he meant that Robin was to get up when he liked on Sunday morning, but the words, never spoken by Aunt Ruby, had a thrilling sound. They were the passwords to freedom, and Robin was so grateful that he cleared away the supper things without being told to do so. Then he washed them up quite well, dried them rather badly, and opened the back door.

From above, through an open window, came the sound of Uncle Dick's snoring.

When Robin reached the recreation ground, he noticed that a rope had been stretched along the length of path that separated it from the road. There was a gap at one end, and beside this sat Mildew Turmut. Beyond her there was a good deal of noise and bustle and excitement. Tent pegs were being hammered into the ground round the Big Top, the show tent of the circus. Really, it was quite a *Little Top* because the Biltong's were not rich and had had many more downs than ups. Altogether, it was rather a scruffy little circus, but what did that matter? Wild blaring music, the most exciting noise in the world, sounded from the merry-go-round. The tarpaulin had been dragged away; horses and ostriches revolved creakily, and went up and down at the same time.

Mildew Turmut flapped her red flag in Robin's face.

'Tickets, please!' she yelled. 'Sixpence entry. Children under twelve half-price, though they did ought to be double, the damage they do – all orange-peel and biscuit crumbs.'

Robin tried to push past, but the stick of the red flag prodded him in the middle.

'Sixpence entry, and it's no use tellin' me you're under twelve.'

Ordinarily Robin would have been flattered at being taken for over twelve. He was rather short for his ten years, so it was a joy to be thought older.

'I *am* under twelve,' he whispered, so that nobody but Mildew could hear (not that anybody else was there to hear). He pulled all his money from his pocket.

'Penalty for defrauding the Railway Companies not exceeding five pounds,' murmured Mildew, but she gave him a used railway ticket: it was from Paddington to Penzance. 'You'll have to get another ticket over there, if you want a ride on the Upper Circle.' She waved her green flag towards the merry-go-round.

Robin simply *had* to show off his knowledge of the London Underground Railways system.

'There's an Inner Circle, and that's not it,' he explained. 'There isn't an Upper Circle.'

'Pardon ME,' Mildew spoke grandly, 'pardon ME, but there *is*. I heard an old gentleman talking about it. Very first class he was – all striped trousers and cigar ash, first-class-corner-seat-reserved. "Us's that moves in Upper Circles," he says very haughty, "us's that moves in the *best* Upper Circles, finds it very annoyin' when second-class standin' passengers rubs their trouser-seats agin the outside o' the first-class carriages. It did ought to be put a stop to," he says. Very first-class cigar ash and coloured silk handkercher in his breast pocket.'

'I oughtn't to pay ANYTHING this evening,' said Robin. 'The circus doesn't begin till Monday.'

'Then stay away!' Mildew turned away to shout to a sparrow who was having a dustbath in the middle of the road. 'Take your ticket for Piccalilli Circus!'

Again Robin *had* to show that he knew something about the world.

'This is Scatterbrook Circus,' he told Mildew and the dusty sparrow. 'Piccadilly Circus is in London, and it isn't a circusy circus!'

For answer, the railway scarecrow jerked her head so furiously that one of her horse-hair plaits flew up and tipped the porter's cap from her head. Out of it (out of the hat, not out of her head) flew a great many tickets – railway tickets, bus tickets, tram tickets, as well as tickets for raffles, and price tickets.

For many years now Mildew Turmut had collected and sorted the sweepings of railway carriages.

'Look for yourself,' she said, 'Piccalilli Circus is printed on one o' them!'

A ticket fluttered on to Robin's shoe, and the letters spelling the word Piccadilly *was* printed on it in black.

Unnoticed by either Robin or Mildew or the sparrow, who continued to cover itself in dust, Upsidaisy trundled up in time to hear the boy's words – 'Anyway, it isn't PiccaLilli – that's a pickle: it's PicaDilly, and that's in London.'

'Anyone as is proper eddicated,' remarked the scarecrow from the school allotments, 'any one as is really proper eddicated, knows as "d" means a penny, and "l" means a pound. If you wants to be learned arithmeticky – a pound's worth more nor a penny, so Piccalilli's worth more nor Piccadilly.'

Robin felt there was something wrong about the argument, but he was not very good at thinking quickly.

Mildew, taking no notice at all of Upsidaisy, shouted again to the sparrow and the sparrow, scattering dust from its wing feathers, zipped up from the road, flew, over the railway scarecrow's head, straight to the elephant, which was being ridden by Worzel Gummidge. Without asking his permission, it tweaked a piece of straw that was sticking out between two of the buttonholes of his shirt.

Sparrows build nests all the year round. This particular sparrow had enjoyed its bath, and felt in a nest-building mood.

Robin followed Upsidaisy as she trundled towards the tent.

'Hannah's practising how she'll sell the Cure-all,' remarked the educated scarecrow.

Mr Biltong, the Fat Lady, Pick-me-up, and Earthy Mangold were all listening to Hannah Harrow, who lolled behind a table, littered with tins, bottles and boxes. As this was a practice performance, and because the crate of Cure-all bottles had not been unpacked there were tins of metal and shoe polish, boxes of matches, and bottles which had held lemonade and turpentine. In a lugubrious voice, she was chanting lists of ailments.

'Cure-all curse blight, rust, mildew and thrush. I've been a cruel sufferer from the thrush. It's a disease what babies gets inside their mouths, and what thrushes has outside o' their chests!' She picked up a ginger-beer bottle and waved it.

The Fat Lady plopped her hands together, and Hannah continued.

'Cure-all cures staggers and stiffness and trembles. Very awkard diseases they are when you get 'em all at once. Stiffness makes you stiff, and staggers makes you stagger. When you staggers stiff all ways at once, you'll maybe fall to pieces. Trembles in the innards is a sign you've got the mice. I've been a cruel sufferer from the mice. Swallerin' mice traps is worse nor no good, seein' they're baited with cheese, so the mice from outside o' you smells it, and joins the mice in the innards.' She raised her voice in a thin scream. 'Cure-all kills mice.'

'Poor little things,' murmured Earthy. 'You'd think they'd have enough to put up with in Hannah's innards without that.'

'Kill-all cures mice!' shouted Hannah Harrow.

'You mustn't say *that*!' The Fat Lady billowed up from the bench she had been over-lapping. 'You mustn't say Kill-all – its Cure-all.'

'Stands to reason, it's the same thing,' said Worzel Gummidge, who was shambling into the tent. 'Kill or cure, it don't make no differ. If it don't kill the mice it'll kill Hannah, and she won't mind the mice.'

The invalid scarecrow, who had been waving her arms, now knocked over a tin of metal polish. A stream of thick white liquid trickled down on to the table. Hannah lowered her head and lapped like a cat. Well, it was not exactly a lapping, it was more like a gulping.

'Very second class!' Mildew Turmut spoke disapprovingly.

'I've heard some makin' that sort o' noise with their soup in dining-carriages when the train stops at stations.'

Hannah continued to mop up the metal polish, and knocked over another large tin of the stuff. Luckily or unluckily, this tin, too, had lost its top.

The Fat Lady turned to her husband.

'Biltong,' she said, 'Biltong, is that the polish you were going to put on the merry-go-round?'

Before he could answer, Hannah Harrow straightened herself. Metal polish was dripping from her tarred boot-lace hair. Dabs of it showed on her face.

'Sopped it up like a medder arter a drought, she did,' said Gummidge. 'She looks like she's revivin' same as grass does.'

A mysterious and sudden change had come over Hannah Harrow. Her voice sounded almost happy. 'Drink Cure-all, and look on the bright side o' things! See what Cure-all's done for me!'

Pick-me-up turned indignantly to the Fat Lady.

'She's using the words I use,' he complained. 'When you took her on to do my work, you said *she* was to act like one that *needed* Cure-all, not like the one that had taken it. She's used my words, and it's not fair!'

He clapped his hand to his swollen cheek.

'And a fat lot of good,' said the Fat Lady, 'a fat lot of good you'd be, standing up with a fat cheek like that, and making out that you'd taken Cure-all.'

'Now, now, NOW!' muttered Mr Biltong soothingly.

'If my cheek's gone down by Monday can I have my job back?' persisted Pick-me-up.

'We'll see about that on Monday,' replied the Fat Lady.

'That's right,' agreed Mr Biltong, who believed in never doing anything that could be put off till tomorrow, or Monday week or many months later.

'Then I'll go to my own caravan till I AM wanted.' Still holding his swollen cheek, Pick-me-up went sulkily out of the tent.

While the argument was continuing, Hannah Harrow had refreshed herself with some more metal polish, for she had found another tin. A strand of boot-lace hair was in her mouth, and she sucked it greedily.

'I don't know what this circus is coming to,' said the Fat Lady. 'I've never known Pick-me-up to be jealous before. If I'm not careful, I'll lose pounds worrying.'

Hannah Harrow let the boot-lace fall from between her lips.

'You did ought to drink Cure-all, then you'll look on the bright side like me. Every cloud's got a silver lining. I feels I wants to shed light and bright all round me like a happy sunbeam.'

'Sunstroke – that's what she's got,' muttered Gummidge. 'Sunstroke – else she's been struck by lightnin'. When trees get struck by lightnin' the bit that's been struck don't grow no leaves. When Hannah moults her hair next autumn—'

Earthy interrupted, 'Hannah's hair don't moult, Worzel, love. It's made o' good hard-wearin' boot-laces.'

Hannah smirked, 'I'll look on the bright side anyways,' she said.

The Fat Lady spoke determinedly, 'You carry on, Biltong, it's time I had another snack and a lay-down, or I'll not be fit to show on Monday.'

Just then the boy who looked after the merry-go-round, and did a great deal of other work as well, rushed into the tent.

'You'd better come quick,' he said, 'the elephant's sitting on your bed and eating your supper!'

How could the elephant have got into the Fat Lady's tent? thought Robin, and Mr Biltong asked the question.

'Stands to reason, it sat on the tent first,' Gummidge told him. 'Very obedient that elephant is!'

'You come along and get it up, Ali Gummidge!' said the Fat Lady. The last elephant trainer in Biltong's Circus had been named Ali, so had the one before.

For a moment Robin hesitated, should he go to the merry-go-round or should he follow the Fat Lady and Mr Biltong and Worzel Gummidge? He decided that the merry-go-round could wait, and that the elephant might not.

As he left the tent he heard Hannah Harrow laughing.

The elephant was sitting on what *had* been the Fat Lady's bed. This was covered with a counterpane that *had* been the tent. Somewhere under this was a tea-chest half full of currant buns. The elephant's trunk had found the way there.

'Sakes!' cried the Fat Lady. 'Just look at the creature!'

The elephant was enjoying itself tremendously: it was very fond of buns. It slid its trunk into the tea-chest and helped itself again.

'Shoo!' cried Mr Biltong mildly. 'Shoo! Shoo!'

The elephant glanced at him disapprovingly, and transferred the bun to its mouth.

'Take it away, Ali Gummidge! Take it away! How can I put it in, and sleep it on, when the elephant's eating what I want to put in, and sitting on the bed I want to lay on?'

'Stands to reason you can't,' said Worzel Gummidge, 'not at the same time as the elephant, you can't. You'll have to take turns. You said I was to look arter the elephant, so I've learned it to look arter itself.'

For once, Mr Biltong did something that *seemed* sensible at first, but, like most of the things he did, it was not really sensible.

As the elephant pushed another bun into its mouth, he grovelled under the wreckage of the tent, and dragged out the tea-chest. Then he hauled it beyond reach of the trunk that was groping towards it.

Very slowly, and with great dignity, the elephant rose from the bed, and lumbered towards the tea-chest.

'Now look what you've done, making it easier for it.'

'You can lay down now, can't you? That's what you wanted, isn't it?'

Mr Biltong tugged at the torn canvas, and uncovered the flattened bed, while the elephant continued to eat buns.

'I can't lay down in the open, can I? It's bad enough having to live in a tent and not in a house!'

'All humans is daft,' remarked Worzel Gummidge. 'They makes houses with doors to keep out the sun. Then they feels cold and sets the houses afire, and knocks holes in the roof to let the smoke out. They're allus makin' work for theirsels.'

'Take that elephant away!' yelled the Fat Lady.

Worzel Gummidge looked at her pityingly.

'You might just as well tell a worm to take a duck away: it happens t'other way on. Stands to reason!'

As though to prove the truth of the words, the elephant, having helped itself to the last bun, curled its trunk round Worzel Gummidge, and lifted him on to its back. Then it turned away, and lumbered towards the merry-go-round.

Robin followed.

The wild music had stopped because the boy who looked after the merry-go-round had been interrupted by the behaviour of the elephant. Now he had gone to look for oil because one of the ostriches creaked rather badly.

'What's come over Hannah?' asked Worzel Gummidge from his high perch.

The invalid scarecrow was behaving very oddly indeed. Somehow she had climbed on to the back of one of the horses, and was rubbing herself against the brass pole above it.

'Why's she rubbin' her back, like as though she was a pig, scratchin' agin a post.'

Hannah turned round, and began to rub her front against the pole. Earthy, who was looking upwards, spoke tenderly, 'Looks like she's in pain, poor thing. Tell us what's the matter, Hannah, love?'

'I'm infectious, that's what I am!' Hannah's voice was oddly cheerful.

'Don't you come near my nelephant then – there's a lot o' it to catch infections. Stands to reason it wouldn't have such a long nose if it weren't liable to catch long bad colds.'

'Out o' door night moths has long noses, too,' remarked

Earthy Mangold. 'Very long noses, they has. I casn't abear to think o' out o' door night moths catchin' bad colds in their spindly noses – nor indeed clothes moths neither.'

Earlier in the day, the mention of moths would have distressed Hannah Harrow, but now she smiled happily.

'Infectious, that's what I am. I feel that bright arter swallerin' Cure-all that everything I touches turns bright.'

It was quite true, as she rubbed her sacking front against the pole, the dingy metal shone as though it had been gilded. The poles on either side of her were gleaming, too.

Her sacking dress was streaked with metal polish. It reminded Robin of the greenish black cloths that were used so often by his Aunt Ruby.

'The way I looks at,' she remarked, 'the brighter you feels the brighter you wants everythink else to look.'

'The teacher says Norma's the brightest girl in the school,' said Upsidaisy, who had been trundling about on the grass.

'If I've any polish left arter I've finished the merry-go-round, I'll bright all the childers up,' said Hannah. 'Now I'll have to start round the other side.'

Obligingly, or perhaps because it liked to exercise its trunk, the elephant picked Hannah up and walked away with her. Then it dumped her on to a horse on the far side of the merry-go-round.

'You'll turn human if you goes on like that, Hannah Harrow,' remarked Gummidge. 'Humans is allus shinin' things bright. They shines winders so's they can see through 'em and then they hangs up curtins so's they can't.'

Although he agreed with Worzel Gummidge, Robin did not want to listen to talk about domestic work. He ran back to Station Cottage. He was terribly tired.

5 Elephant Rings

'There's not been half a to-doing,' remarked Uncle Dick, as Robin stumbled sleepily into the kitchen at quarter to twelve on the very same Sunday morning.

'I gave you a shake, but you were sleeping so sound, I didn't like to wake you.'

How lucky it was that Aunt Ruby was in London! She would have been horrified at the sight of a boy asleep in all his clothes, with dust and grass stains rubbed *off* them and *on to* a clean honeycomb quilt.

'You don't often see an elephant lying across the railway lines,' continued Uncle Dick.

He was cooking the Sunday dinner – sausages and eggs and bacon because Aunt Ruby had thought, quite rightly, that he and Robin were not to be trusted with a joint.

'I mightn't have noticed it myself, but Bert happened to come back. He'd left his football coupons in the ticket office, and came back to fetch them. He happened to notice the elephant.'

Uncle Dick turned a piece of bacon in the frying pan.

He had not bothered to prick the sausages, and they had split, showing black frilly edges. The insides were bursting out of their skins. They were just as Robin liked them.

As a matter of fact, he would have liked anything that morning.

It is one of the queer laws of nature, that, though you need nothing to eat through the night if you are asleep, if you are awake you need breakfast, supper, dinner and tea.

'I gave it a carrot but that wasn't any good,' said Uncle Dick.

Robin understood in the way that man and man, and boy and boy, or man and boy do understand the short conversations in which very few words are spoken.

He knew that his uncle, remembering the old-time method of making a donkey *go*, had dangled a carrot before the elephant's nose, and that the beast had refused to be interested.

'Was anyone with it?' he asked.

'Not that I noticed.'

Uncle Dick cracked one egg after another against the edge of the frying-pan, and the yolks broke, too. (Aunt Ruby would never have allowed *that* to happen. Her fried eggs were neat and tidy: their yolks glared up like yellow eyes in the middle of the dull uninteresting white.) Uncle Dick stirred the eggs into a glorious sizzling shemozzle of yellow and crispy white on to the top of the bacon.

'A fat woman and a thin man came along after Bert fetched them. She took the elephant back to the circus, and Bert found his football coupons.'

Uncle Dick stirred the mixture in the frying-pan.

'They were looking for someone – a chap called Ali Something. He was a black chap, in with a gang, I reckon. I'm not much of a cook,' he added.

He seemed the best cook in the world to Robin, who must, surely, have been the hungriest boy in it.

When they were half way through the glorious meal, Uncle Dick put down his knife and fork.

'Yes, there was quite a to-doing over that black chap and his gang. I told 'em, I read about him in the Sunday papers or somewhere. Ali – Ali – Something?'

Uncle Dick raised his thick fist, and pounded it down on to a harmless wasp that was exploring a pot of blackcurrant jam on the table.

'Got it!' he shouted.

'Ali Baba! He was in with a gang of forty thieves, and he hid 'em in big pots the size of milk-churns. I read it in the Sunday papers or somewhere.'

The whole of a fairy story drifted into Robin's mind. He had been reminded of it before by the sight of the milk-churns on Scatterbrook station. The thieves inside could pop up their heads, and the milk-churn lids could make hats for them – sort of crash helmets.

He nodded.

'Ali Baba and the Forty Thieves.'

'They said he was in with a gang,' agreèd Uncle Dick. 'We've only bananas for afters. Your Aunty said you'd to go to Sunday School with Marlene.'

Half an hour afterwards Marlene arrived. She was wearing her best blue frock, and she spoke importantly.

'We've only to have short Sunday School. Then we've to go to the downs with Miss Dollit.'

'That one!' said Uncle Dick.

'You and me are to go to Mrs Bloomsbury-Barton when we've come back from the downs,' added Marlene.

'That one!' said Uncle Dick. 'Then you'd best go and wash, else I'll cop it from your Aunt.'

As Robin dashed for the bathroom, he added, 'The best way to make hair look right in a hurry's a wet brush. Hair doesn't spring up for a bit *after* a wet brush. Better take this.'

He handed a scrubbing brush to Robin, and added, 'It does for knees, too.'

Good old Uncle Dick! thought Robin in the bathroom, as he scoured the grass-stains from his knees.

Marlene was waiting for him on the platform.

'Come on,' said Robin.

Miss Dollit was in charge of the Sunday School but, as she had promised, she did not keep the children for very long.

At the end of the last hymn, she shut the piano lid with a bang, and stood up.

'Now,' she cried, 'I've a treat for all of you – a perfectly lovely treat! Who would like to come up to the downs with me, and look for fairy rings?'

All the boys, and most of the girls, sat quite still.

'Hands up! Hands up, all of you who would like to come.'

Several of the little girls put their hands up.

'Robin Elliot *must* come because he and Marlene have been chosen by Mrs Bloomsbury-Barton for an extra special treat afterwards.'

Obediently, Robin raised a hand – his left one because the other was busy with the Plasticine in his right-hand pocket.

Another little boy shot both hands up above his head.

'I'll tell you all about it as we go,' she said. 'You can put your hands down now, Cyril: I know you want to come.'

Robin had hoped they might go by way of the recreation ground, but Miss Dollit had chosen another path, skirting the field where the merry-go-round and caravans and tents had been arranged.

She continued to prattle. 'I saw the fairy rings this morning when I took Mrs Bloomsbury-Barton's little doggy for a walk after church. Doggies must go for walks, mustn't they, even on Sundays? One of these rings went right through a gap in the hedge. The poor fairies must have scratched their wings badly, I should think, when they danced between the thorns. The grass in one field was quite bruised and battered, only luckily the hay harvest is in. And there were some most enormous footprints as well as tiny ones. Perhaps the tiny ones were made by a fairy deer. What do you think, kiddies?'

Nobody answered, but Robin listened hard. Could the rings have been made by the elephant?

Miss Dollit continued, 'The other footmarks must have been made by fairy giants, don't you think?'

'P'raps they were made by angels!' suggested Marlene, memories of Sunday School still with her.

'Oh, I don't think so, dear.'

Because they were climbing, and the downs were steep, and she was becoming rather breathless, Miss Dollit did not speak again until they reached the place where the elephant had obviously rested.

'That isn't a fairy ring, dear, you'll have to be patient for just a little longer. Dear! Dear! How crushed the grass is. I should think some big cow has been lying on it.'

'A cow as big as an elephant,' remarked Marlene.

How could she know that? wondered Robin.

'If an elephant had been lying there I might find some of its hairs and make them into rings and sell them,' said Marlene. 'Elephant hairs are ever so lucky.'

'You won't find an elephant hair here, dear!' laughed Miss Dollit.

How little she knew! thought Robin.

The turf was firm, and the elephant's feet had made no marks on its close-cropped surface.

'There!' cried Miss Dollit when they had reached the top of the ridge, 'there!'

And there below them were the great trampled circles showing dark green among the paler green of the newly cut hayfield. The outer ones had made the gaps in the hedges wider. Luckily none had reached the standing corn.

Farmer Braithewaite, who liked to walk round his fields on Sunday afternoons, and wanted, also, to make sure that none of the circus people were lighting what he called 'their gipsy fires', was plodding slowly up the downs from the Scatterbrook side.

'Well!' he said, as he reached Miss Dollit's side. 'Look at that *now*!'

'They are looking at the fairy rings!' explained Miss Dollit. 'It's wonderful what an interest they are taking *now*.'

'Fairy rings!' almost shouted the farmer. 'I should think they're making elephant rings more like.'

'No, no, they're not making them: they're only following them round. The rings were there *before*.'

'Not yesterday – they weren't. I was all round those fields myself. You can't trust these gipsy types not to break down the hedges for their fires. If we get rain in time, I might have had a second hay crop – *might* have.'

'But *really*—' began Miss Dollit.

Cyril was standing in the very middle of a gap. His best jacket was hitched on to a thorn.

'Hi! You!' shouted Farmer Braithewaite. 'You, boy! Come out of that at once, and all the rest of you.'

Cyril started, and the thorn ripped his jacket.

Some of the children straggled up the slope. Others decided to take short cuts home so that they should not be recognized by the farmer, who had a habit of complaining to parents.

Miss Dollit did her best to soothe Mr Braithewaite. 'I always think there is so much in the world that we don't understand.'

'I understand broken down hedges all right.'

'But *really* they were broken down before by – well, by something mysterious. You would have seen that for yourself if you had come a little earlier.'

'I came soon enough to see *that*.' The farmer waved his stick towards the elephant tracks.

'They were *just* like fairy rings early this morning before any of the children were here.'

'Fairy rings!' snorted the farmer, and Robin arrived on the ridge just in time to hear him. 'If you said they were like elephant rings you'd be nearer the mark.'

Poor Miss Dollit looked so sad and so flustered and the farmer looked so scornful and so angry that Robin simply could not help saying what he did.

'As a matter of fact, they *are* elephant rings!'

'I don't want any sauce from you, my lad,' snapped the farmer.

And then, from below on the recreation ground, rose the sound of trumpeting. It was faint and muffled by distance, but it was an unusual noise to be heard in Scatterbrook on a Sunday afternoon.

The farmer swung round, so did Miss Dollit, and so did Robin.

There, looking like a toy, because it was so far away, the merry-go-round glittered in the sunlight. Beside it stood the elephant, lonely and bored. It waved its trunk and trumpeted again.

'Well, I'll be jiggered!' exclaimed the farmer, 'so there *is* a loose elephant. I'll soon see about that. Afternoon, Miss Dollit.'

He hurried downhill towards the recreation ground.

'*And now*,' thought Robin miserably, 'I *have* done it.'

He had saved Miss Dollit from the farmer's rage, but the Fat Lady or poor Mr Biltong or Worzel Gummidge or all three would get into trouble. He remembered some sad words of Earthy Mangold's, 'It's complicate to try to comfort spiders *and* flies at the same time.'

'You clever little boy!' said Miss Dollit. 'However did you guess? And now we had better go to Mrs Bloomsbury-Barton.'

6 Aunt Sally

Mrs Bloomsbury-Barton was waiting for them in the garden of the White House.

'You are not very tidy, are you?' she said, looking disapprovingly at Marlene's crumpled frock, Robin's grassy knees, and at his red hair which was standing almost on end.

It was quite true: they were not at all tidy. Robin did not care for Mrs Bloomsbury-Barton's fluffy, flimsy frock or high-heeled shoes or flowery hat either. Grown-up people can say things to children about their clothes, but children must be polite.

He scowled, and rubbed one shoe against the other.

'Don't fidget!' said Mrs Bloomsbury-Barton. Then she turned to Miss Dollit.

'Really, Phoebe, you look as flushed as though you had been running races! I hope these children are the *right* ones to be trusted with this particular errand.'

So it was to be an errand, was it? Miss Dollit had said there was to be a treat.

Now she was speaking in her usual flurried way, 'I thought we agreed that as Robin lives at Station Cottage, he could leave the barrow at the station overnight, and then Bert could wheel it up in the morning with the little girl's luggage. We *did* agree, Mrs Bloomsbury-Barton. You said it would be killing two birds with one stone.' She turned to the children, and added, 'That's only an expression, of course – Mrs Bloomsbury-Barton would never dream of throwing stones at birds!'

'Can I have a drink of water, please?' asked Marlene.

'You should never drink water when you are over-hot.' Mrs Bloomsbury-Barton peered down at the children, and Marlene wiped her face with a handkerchief so that she would look cooler.

Perhaps, thought Robin, perhaps if it were bad for hot children to drink *water*, she would offer them some lemonade.

She did nothing so kind, but said, 'Very well, but remember to sip the water slowly. Run along, you'll find Mrs Marble in the kitchen.'

'And we'll get her out while they're gone, and put her in the wheel-barrow,' said Miss Dollit. 'What fun it will be for them!'

Who could this person be? wondered Robin, and why must she be put into a wheel-barrow? Was she lame? Why would it be fun?

Mrs Marble, who came sometimes to help Mrs Bloomsbury-Barton, poured some rather tepid water into a couple of cups, and grumbled as she did so.

'I don't hold with pandering to gipsies,' she complained. 'If you ask me it's asking for trouble. Once let one of them get a foot inside the house, and Mrs Bloomsbury-Barton's silver will be stolen, let alone the Whitby jet my aunt left me. AND we'll be murdered in our beds, like as not. You can't trust gipsies, though they do say the mahogany and bright-work in their caravan's polished up. Mind you don't let them know which house it comes from when you take it along. Just you leave it and come away.'

'Leave what?' asked Marlene, putting down her cup.

'That old image.'

Sometimes when Marlene's mother was rather cross with her, she called her daughter 'a naughty little image'.

Supposing an image was some sort of imp – 'an imp of mischief'. Marlene looked interested.

'What image?' Robin asked.

'You'll see soon enough – it's that old Aunt Sally of hers.'

It was difficult to think of Mrs Bloomsbury-Barton as having an aunt. Robin wondered why she was to be put into a barrow and wheeled to the recreation ground.

'Don't you let those gipsies know which house it comes from,' repeated Mrs Marble. 'I daresay they'll try to wheedle it out of you, and then we'll all be murdered. If you ask me, Mrs Bloomsbury-Barton's a great deal too kind-hearted. Off you go now, out of my kitchen. I've plenty to do as it is.'

Miss Dollit and Mrs Bloomsbury-Barton were talking together on the lawn. Between them stood a creature who, certainly, was no relation of any human. She was made of wood, and her nose stuck out sharply from her hard bright face. Like Upsidaisy, she had three legs. She wore an old-fashioned frock, patterned with yellow daisies, and a bonnet was perched on her painted wooden hair. Her mouth was primmed up into an O, and in it was a pipe.

'I've seen it before at the village fêtes,' whispered Marlene. 'You throw sticks at it – three sticks for a penny, and the one that hits it wins a prize. Its front leg's hinged: I've looked under its skirt.'

Mrs Bloomsbury-Barton glanced round.

'Say anything you wish to say out loud. Don't you know it's rude to whisper? Now listen to me.'

She explained then that she was sorry for the circus people – 'Such a wretched little circus.'

Her words made Robin feel that it was the very best circus in the world. It had an elephant and a merry-go-round, and sea-lions and a Fat Lady, as well as the Scatterbrook scarecrows for helpers.

'I had a chat with that most unfortunately fat woman, and I understand they have had serious trouble with some of their workers.'

Robin glanced at Marlene, and she glanced back at him.

'Please *look* at me when I am speaking,' snapped Mrs Bloomsbury-Barton. 'As I was saying, I felt so sorry for the poor things with their *wretched* little circus that I offered to lend them my Aunt Sally. Perhaps if they set it up, they may make a few extra coppers. Please ask them to take the very greatest care of it. Phoebe, will you get the wheel-barrow?'

Between them, Miss Dollit and Mrs Bloomsbury-Barton arranged the Aunt Sally on the wheel-barrow. Her hinged leg creaked horridly, and her face looked even shinier and harder than it had done before.

All the time this was happening Mrs Bloomsbury-Barton gave her orders. The children were not to worry the circus people. They were to leave the empty barrow at the station. ('Bert will bring it back tomorrow when he wheels up my little niece's luggage.') They were not to stare at the Fat Lady. They were not to go near the merry-go-round. They could tell Mr Biltong that Mrs Bloomsbury-Barton would send for the scarecrow at the end of the week.

'And now,' she added, 'you can take the Aunt Sally's pipe and put it safely in your pocket. Don't forget to give it to Mr Biltong. I am speaking to *you*, little boy.'

Robin tugged gently at the pipe, and then tugged harder.

'It won't come out,' he said, 'she's biting it.'

'Nonsense!' Mrs Bloomsbury-Barton wrenched the pipe from the Aunt Sally's mouth and pushed it into Robin's pocket.

'Now you can wheel the barrow, and Marlene can steady the Aunt Sally. Don't be rough with it.'

It was the Aunt Sally who was rough.

As Robin was wheeling the barrow along the road, Marlene gave a little yelp.

'It's your turn to hold her now,' she said. 'I'll push.'

'Why?' asked Robin.

'Because!' replied Marlene, who was rubbing her fore-arm, and looking in a frightened way at the Aunt Sally.

A few minutes after they had changed places, Robin felt a sudden mouse-trappish nip on his elbow.

Aunt Sally did not look either pleased or sorry. She stared up at the sky.

'Got you?' asked Marlene.

Robin did not answer: he was feeling too puzzled.

'Tell you what,' said Marlene, as she set down the barrow legs on the road outside Finch Cottage. 'Let's put her up in your garden. The circus doesn't begin until tomorrow. We can call some of the others and charge them six throws a halfpenny. Let's put her up in your garden, and come back after tea.'

The words 'your garden' made Robin feel very important indeed.

'All right.' He strode to the gate, and opened it.

They set the Aunt Sally up in a waste piece of ground in the back garden. There were no more pinchings, but when they had finished, she jerked out an arm, snatched the pipe (its stem was sticking out of Robin's pocket), and popped it into her mouth.

It happened so quickly that neither of the children felt absolutely certain that it *had* happened. Only – the pipe was there in her mouth!

'Did *you*—' began both children together, and then stopped. Sometimes it is better not to ask questions. Sometimes it is better to take no notice at all.

'Just going to see if the sitting-room window's open,' said Robin, and, with Marlene following, he dashed round to the front of the cottage.

The window was tightly shut.

'Let's go and look down at HER from an upstair window,' said Marlene. She turned the front door handle, and walked inside.

That was queer enough because Robin was absolutely certain that he had locked the door yesterday. (Could it be only yesterday?) The inside of the cottage was queerer still.

The whole of one kitchen wall was covered with a huge drawing of a spider's web. A heap of soot in the grate, some straws from a bottle-straw boot and an old besom (at least it had been a besom – now it was a broom handle with two or three twigs left on it) – made Robin guess the names of the artists.

On another wall there were portraits of the scarecrows – Earthy Mangold and Hannah Harrow. These had been filled in solidly with soot. In their way, they were quite good likenesses.

'That's done it!' said Robin.

'I knew you'd be pleased.'

Earthy Mangold was speaking from the doorway leading into the scullery.

'Mr Gummidge drawed us, and we drawed him. We did him in the other room.'

'How?' asked Robin.

'We stood up agin the wall, and Mr Gummidge drawed round us with a bottle-straw dipped in soot. He swep' the chimley o' purpose to get a lot o' soot. Arter he'd drawed us, we rubbed the soot all over our shapes. We got some furnyture, too. I knowed you'd be pleased!'

Earthy's kind little face was full of love and happiness.

'It were a surprise!' she added.

It was, thought Robin, a surprise all right!

There was furniture of a sort in the kitchen. A broken chicken-coop stood in the middle of the kitchen. Beside it was a deck chair without any canvas and a roll of rusty wire-netting. Robin remembered that these had been left on the rubbish heap when his Aunt Ruby moved from Finch cottage. Bits of broken china, flower-pots and a spoutless teapot were ranged on the mantelshelf.

'I knowed you'd like some ornyments!' said Earthy. 'Aren't you pleased?'

Robin could not bear to hurt her feelings: his own had been hurt too often when he had planned surprises for grown-up people. He said the only thing he could think of.

'It's smashing!'

'We had to smash the frame a bit to make the bed,' Earthy waved a twiggy hand towards a corner of the kitchen. 'Hannah said frames is the proper covers for hot beds, seein' humans need to keep warm at night.'

On a litter of earth and straw and old leaves lay a battered cucumber frame without any glass. Hannah Harrow, moaning faintly, lay on this.

'She thought, maybe, you'd not mind sharin' the bed with her, seein' she's so delikit,' said Earthy. 'Come along o' me, and see Mr Gummidge's picter now. He wouldn't have it on the same wall with us acos he said it needed to be alone to sulk. It's differ from our ones.'

Half shuffling, half hopping, Earthy led the way into the sitting-room.

Worzel Gummidge's portrait *was* quite different. It was simply enormous. The head with the billy-cock hat reached almost up to the ceiling. The broomstick arms stretched from one wall to another.

'We had to draw him with the besom,' explained Earthy. 'We couldn't reach with the bottle-straws. Mr Gummidge made us draw him sulkin'. We couldn't draw *round* him neither acos he wanted to look so big. He stood out in the middle, and we drawed round his shadder.'

Worzel Gummidge himself was sitting in a deck chair, and admiring his portrait. No, he was not exactly sitting because this chair, like the one in the kitchen, had no canvas. He was sitting on the floor, and his legs were sprawled outside the frame.

'It's very big,' said Robin, thinking he must say something because Earthy looked so very proud of herself.

'Stands to reason!' said Gummidge. 'It's a drawin' o' me shadder. Shadders is big, but they goes away at sunset. This one'll stay for ever and ever and ever to remind me o' me.'

Robin thought sadly of his Aunt Ruby, and Earthy broke into the conversation.

'I wunner where shadders goes at sunset.'

'Most like somethin' eats 'em!' said Gummidge.

'Oh, Worzel, love!' Earthy broke into a flood of green tears, 'I casn't abear to think o' no one eatin' your shadders – not unless they was starvin'.'

'No one won't eat this shadder. Stands to reason!'

Robin wished that somebody could eat it, or cover it up or hide it *somehow* before his parents moved into Finch Cottage.

'We might rub it off with bread,' whispered Marlene. 'We could get one of the stale loaves the baker gives Mrs Kibbins for her hens.'

Earthy dabbed her eyes with a banana-skin handkerchief, and looked quite cheerful again.

'Shadders is very complicate,' she remarked. 'You'd think they'd be smaller nor the things they're shadders of.'

'Stands to reason my shadder's big,' boasted Gummidge. 'It's as big as I feels. I'll not have no little shadders sulkin' about, and makin' a mock o' me.'

'If shadders o' flies was big, and shadders o' spiders was little, it'd be a lot kinder,' said Earthy thoughtfully. 'Then the shadders o' the flies couldn't be ate up by the shadders o' spiders.'

'Then the shadders o' the spiders'd be ate by the shadders o' the flies,' argued Gummidge. 'There's a lot more flies nor there is spiders, so the shadders o' flies'd starve when they'd ate up all the spiders. Stands to reason!'

At that sad thought, Earthy began to sob again. Robin felt that he could have cried, too – not out of pity for the starving shadows of flies but because he knew his parents, particularly his mother, would not care for the portrait of Worzel Gummidge.

There was an interruption. Hannah Harrow, whimpering wretchedly, dragged herself into the sitting-room.

'A moth come at me!' she moaned. 'I'll not lay there alone with moths eatin' my heart.'

'Stands to reason if moths is there, you're not alone,' said

Gummidge. He added rudely, 'Any moth as wasn't daft'd sooner be alone nor with you.'

'Let me wipe that bit o' cobweb off of your face, Hannah, love – else you'll get moths flutteratin' in it.'

As Earthy pulled out her banana-skin handkerchief, some small round things rattled down on to the floor.

'Thems for you,' she said to Robin. 'I found 'em on the rubbige heap.'

A queer half musty smell drifted up from the floor. It was the smell of his mother's winter coat when she took it out of its cardboard box at the end of summer.

'Thems for you,' repeated Earthy. 'I know human boys likes to play marbles.'

'They're moth balls!' cried Marlene, swooping down on them.

'I didn't know as moths played ball,' Earthy looked puzzled.

'They're to keep moths away,' explained Marlene.

As the little girl stood there, a couple of grubby moth balls lying in her outstretched palm, Hannah Harrow made a curious ducking movement of her head. Marlene yelped, and the moth balls were gone. They had been swallowed by the invalid scarecrow!

There came a rat-tatting at the front door, and the bright voice of Miss Dollit calling 'Is anyone in?'

Robin and Marlene rushed into the kitchen. Miss Dollit was there already.

'I saw the wheel-barrow outside,' she explained. 'You *have* been quick. I shouldn't have thought you could have got to the recreation ground and back in such a very short time. I've just been taking a lemon sponge to the policeman's mother: she hasn't been very well, poor dear.'

Robin slammed the door leading into the sitting-room, and stood with his back against it.

'So this is to be your new home, Robin. I see you and Marlene have been playing houses.'

Miss Dollit glanced at the chicken-coop and the deck chair, then she looked at the drawing of the spider's web and the portraits of Earthy and Hannah.

Stepping back, and nearly tripping over the wire netting, she asked, 'Did you do these?'

'No,' answered Marlene quickly.

Robin shuffled his feet, and looked down at the floor. Now for it! he thought.

'But they are wonderful! Quite wonderful!'

Miss Dollit pranced round the room. She kept stepping backwards and putting her head on one side.

'They are like the primitive drawings in old caves – the untaught work of savages. I didn't know you were an artist, Robin. Have any of your teachers seen these?'

'No,' he mumbled, hoping they never would.

'But they MUST. They ought to see them. You mustn't be so modest, Robin! I shall run down to the school tomorrow – no, I mayn't be free tomorrow – the day after – and ask Mr Kimber to come up and look at them. They are just like the primitive drawings in caves.'

Robin remembered having been shown photographs of drawings – elephants and other beasts – made in pre-historic caves, and had not thought much of them.

'I suppose these were done as a surprise for your parents?'

Robin nodded.

'Such a good idea! How pleased your mother will be.'

He doubted it. His mother liked pretty wall-papers with spriggy patterns, and she liked pretty pictures of pretty places.

'Well, I shall bring Mr Kimber up the day after tomorrow' (that was bad!) 'and I shall tell him that I don't think you ought to be *taught* at all!' (That was good! He most particularly hated arithmetic.) 'I mean, you should not be taught drawing or painting.' (That was not quite so good: he rather liked splodging about with paints!) 'I think you are a natural artist, but that must not make you conceited.' (He did not feel in the very least conceited: he felt in the most dreadful muddle.)

'By the way,' added Miss Dollit. 'By the way, did the Circus people tell you they were pleased with the Aunt Sally?'

'No,' said Robin, after a pause. It was true, but he did not feel that it was true. He did not feel very happy (and in many more ways than one) about the scarecrow pictures either. If they were good, then he should not be praised for them. But how *could* he explain about the Gummidges.

'Well,' said Miss Dollit, 'I expect you'd better take the barrow back to the station now, and I must skip back to tea.'

Robin was hungry, too, and so was Marlene.

It was much better to wheel an empty barrow than one that was full of Aunt Sally.

Robin was glad when he reached Station Cottage.

Directly after he had had his tea, Robin hurried back to Finch Cottage.

The cottage door was wide open, and there were no scarecrows in kitchen or sitting-room – only the 'furniture' and the pictures and a faint smell of moth-balls.

He ran into the back garden.

Aunt Sally was there, but she had moved or had been moved from the place where they had left her, and was now much nearer to the rubbish heap where the three scarecrows sat in a disconsolate row. They looked like children who are being scolded, and they *were* being scolded.

The stem of Aunt Sally's pipe was sticking out of the pocket in her flowery frock. She spoke in a hard wooden voice, and at the end of every sentence she pursed up her mouth into a horrid round O.

'Worzel,' she was saying, 'I intend to be obeyed.'

'Ooh aye!' replied Gummidge sulkily.

'That is no way to answer. You should say, "Yes, Aunt".'

'Beggin' your pardon,' said Earthy Mangold, very politely indeed. 'Beggin' your pardon, and if it's all the same to you, I'm Worzel's wife now, so you casn't be his aunt.'

'Stands to reason,' muttered Worzel Gummidge. 'Earthy couldn't a been my wife – not unless I'd agreed, and you couldn't a been my aunt unless I'd agreed. I've disagreed now, and you can stop bein' a aunt.'

'I'd a lady friend once as suffered from aunts,' moaned Hannah Harrow. 'She happened to have a flour-sack skin, and her stuffin' was made o' sugar bags. One day she happened to lay down on a aunt-hill, and the aunts got at her somethink cruel. There was hunderds and hunderds o' nasty little aunts crawlin' all over her. It makes me feel bad to think o' it – not that I wasn't feelin' bad afore.'

'Nonsense, Hannah. You are perfectly well! You need to be taken out of yourself,' snapped Aunt Sally.

'Scarecrows should be seen and not heard.'

Aunt Sally pursed her lips into an O, and Gummidge said,

'Stands to reason, Hannah's not *worth* lookin' at.'

'Do not make personal remarks, Worzel.'

Aunt Sally moved forward. Her hinged leg stepped jerkily; the other two dragged after it.

'I intend to take up my residence here. Give me the key at once, and without further argument.'

The shock of those words made Robin forget to be frightened of Aunt Sally.

'You can't!' he shouted. 'You can't live here!'

'Speak when you're spoken to!' said Aunt Sally, but she stopped walking. 'This cottage does not belong to you.'

'It does. Well, *partly* it does.'

'Then we will share it. There is not nearly enough give and take in the world. You will be a very different little boy by the time I have finished with you. Why did you bring me here if you did not intend me to stay?'

Very slowly and creakily, Worzel Gummidge rose from the rubbish heap, and began to shamble away.

'Stop!'

Aunt Sally spoke in the kind of voice that not even a scarecrow dared to disobey. 'Where are you going?'

'Back to my work. Back to my nelephant. I'm a nelephant trainer now.'

'Then give me the key of the cottage, Robin,' said Aunt Sally.

Aunt Sally was glaring. Her eyes looked almost as round as her mouth. The hinge of her front leg squeaked as she stepped forward.

Robin dashed round to the front of Finch Cottage, slammed and locked the door behind him, and ran upstairs. Somehow, he did not care for the idea of being alone on the ground floor, for fear Aunt Sally should smash a window with her sharp nose or her pipe or horridly-hinged front leg.

Five minutes later he watched a curious procession making its way through a gap in the elder hedge behind the rubbish heap.

Worzel Gummidge went first, shambling and shuffling. After him came Earthy Mangold, hopping along in a birdlike way. Hannah, although she sagged and drooped, moved much more quickly than usual. There was a reason for this: Aunt Sally was following. She jerked through the elder hedge, and walked with a curious tilting movement. Robin noticed that her pipe was in her mouth. At least, she would not be able to scold the others when she caught up with them.

He guessed they would make their way, by fields and hedges, to the recreation ground. What would happen to them there, he wondered, but he did not wonder for very long. He had had almost enough of scarecrows for one day.

7 The End of a Circus

It was half-past five, and at six o'clock the Circus was due to begin. A group of children, Robin and Marlene among them, stood outside the rope dividing the recreation ground from the path. Another bit of rope had been joined to it, so that the entrance was closed.

Nobody shouted 'Tickets, please!' and no music sounded from the merry-go-round which had been covered with its tarpaulin.

'They'll have to look sharp if they're going to begin at six,' said Marlene.

The elephant was mooning about alone. The Big Top lay on the ground among a tangle of poles and guy-ropes. The sea-lions' voices rose sadly in the distance. The Fat Lady sat outside her tent. She was stirring something in a saucepan on top of a primus stove.

It seemed a very odd beginning to a circus.

Pick-me-up, his face still swollen slightly, hurried over to the barrier and spoke to the children.

'You kids can hop it. We're not opening tonight. We're on the move!'

'Why?' asked Robin.

'Ask him, not me!' Pick-me-up jerked a thumb towards Mr Biltong, who was sitting on the steps of a caravan. His hands dangled in front of him, and his hat was pulled over his face, as though, like an ostrich, he hoped not to be seen so long as his head was covered completely.

'Ask old man Biltong. He ONLY came to the wrong place. He only sent advance notices to Scatterbrook when they should have gone to Penfold. He only hired such a set of scallywags as never was, and hasn't the money to pay them off because he's lost the cash box! They've sent over from Penfold to ask why we're not there!'

Pick-me-up paused for breath.

'Ask old man Biltong why we're on the move, and see what he says. She' – he pointed towards the Fat Lady – 'she's been asking for long enough!'

Steam rose up from the saucepan on the primus stove. The Fat Lady dipped a spoon into the mixture and tasted it.

Some of the children surged forward, pressing against the rope.

'Oh no, you don't!' said Pick-me-up. 'We've enough to do without having a lot of kiddies messing round.'

'There's a good picture on at Dimden,' said Norma to Tommy Higginsthwaite. 'Let's get our bikes and go.'

Most of the children followed her, and Pick-me-up, in answer to a shout from the Fat Lady, turned away.

Only Robin and Marlene were left.

'Come on in,' she said. 'It's the last chance of getting some elephant hairs.'

Robin was not interested in elephant hairs, but he did want to find the scarecrows. He noticed that the elephant had picked up a bottle-straw boot with its trunk, and was waving it about.

The two children ducked under the rope, ran across the grass, and dodged behind the Fat Lady's tattered tent as they heard her shout, 'Hi! You!'

She was not speaking to them but to Mr Biltong, who left the caravan steps, and walked sadly towards her. Pick-me-up, hurrying away, met him, stopped and said something that made poor Mr Biltong look sadder than ever.

'Now have you thought where you hid the cash box?' asked the Fat Lady as her husband, looking ashamed as a puppy that has chewed up a slipper, joined her. 'You've had time enough in all conscience.'

The children, peeping through some slits in the ragged tent, watched him, and felt sorry as they waited for his answer.

'It's come back to me now, I buried it to keep it safe.'

'You buried it to keep it safe!' The Fat Lady spooned up some more stew. 'Where did you bury it?'

'That's just it. I buried it somewhere round about – somewhere not far from the middle, I *think* it was.'

'You *think* it was! You *think* it was! But you didn't think to mark the place, I suppose?'

'That's just it, I did *mark* it.'

'Where's the mark then?'

'The mark's gone,' confessed Mr Biltong.

'Where?'

'All over the place. It went all over the place afterwards.'

'What sort of a mark was it, then?'

'It was – it was the elephant.'

The Fat Lady choked, partly from rage and partly because she had swallowed some very hot stew.

'It was lying down, you see, and I thought to myself, "It's big enough, and if I bury the cash box by its trunk, I'll find it again easy." I'd wanted to hide it under your bed same as I do sometimes, but you were asleep and you don't like being disturbed when you're sleeping it on. I'd meant to dig it up when you woke, and then—'

'Then what?'

'Then the elephant had gone. I didn't think—'

'Oh yes, you did!' said the Fat Lady. 'You thought the elephant was a statue. You thought it'd lay there for ever like one of those lions in Trafalgar Square. You didn't think it'd move, oh no!'

'I didn't think it'd wake so soon. I didn't think you'd wake so soon either. It was you shouting out about all those tins of metal polish being empty that put it out of my head.'

It was unfortunate that Mr Biltong should have mentioned the metal polish because the Fat Lady, after strengthening herself with more stew, began to rage again.

'I'd think you'd be ashamed to mention metal polish. About the only job you ever did in your life was to polish up the merry-go-round – *if* you did do it.' (Robin knew that Mr Biltong had *not* done the polishing.) 'You used enough polish to keep an elephant in liquor for a fortnight.'

Mr Biltong glanced doubtfully at the elephant which was meandering about, and still carrying Worzel Gummidge's bottle-straw boot.

'And how,' asked the Fat Lady, 'how are we to pay Ali, and all the other freaks you hired? I'm not taking them along with us to Penfold, that's very sure and certain. If we can't pay them, they'll come. They're over there by the side of the merry-go-round, and looking very ugly. They're having a meeting, I daresay. Very ugly they look!'

The scarecrows – Worzel Gummidge, Earthy Mangold, Hannah Harrow, Mildew Turmut and Upsidaisy – were standing in a dishevelled group near the merry-go-round. Beside them was Aunt Sally.

It would, thought Robin, be dreadful if they (except Aunt Sally) decided to leave Scatterbrook. He nudged Marlene, and whispered, 'Let's find out what's happening.'

As they ran over the trampled grass, the Fat Lady shouted, 'Hi, you!' They stopped, and she beckoned to them with a mighty hand. 'Hi! You! Come here!'

'She's going to remember about the sea-lions,' muttered Marlene, 'and about me wanting to jump through hoops.'

However, the Fat Lady showed no sign of remembering.

'The circus is closed,' she said. 'What do you want?'

'We thought,' replied Robin, thinking of it for the first time. 'We thought we could look for the cash box.'

'That's right,' nodded Mr Biltong.

'You might as well look for my funny bone!'

The Fat Lady raised an enormous and dimpled elbow as

she dipped her spoon into the stew. 'You'd have as much chance of finding it. Still, there's no harm in trying. Not that you won't find my funny bone easy enough if this sort of thing goes on. I'll be a living skeleton before I've done with circuses.'

'Now then, ducks, you've been putting it on famously!' said Mr Biltong.

As a dog responds to being called 'Good dog', the Fat Lady's smile answered to the word *ducks*.

'Go along with you!' she said, speaking to her husband.

The children obeyed, and, as they went, they heard a spoon scraping hopefully round the inside of a saucepan.

There was no chance of finding a buried cash box under the turf of the recreation ground. The grass was much too battered and bruised, too dented by elephant foot-prints and tent pegs.

They scuffled about for a little, prodding the earth with their toes, and kicking with their heels.

'No go!' said Robin and, as he walked towards the group of scarecrows, Earthy Mangold came, hoppingly, to meet him.

'We're goin' to have a circus to oursels,' she said. 'We'll have performin' fleas an' all sorts.'

'Ooh aye!' Worzel Gummidge limped forward.

The children noticed that he was wearing one bottle-straw boot, his other broomstick ankle was bare except for the earth and grass-roots encrusted round it.

'That daft Pick-me-up were sayin' as all proper circuses has performin' fleas. Mrs Kibbin's hens has plenty o' fleas. We'll fetch a hen from out o' her hen-house.'

'Performing fleas are trained,' began Robin, who had once seen some of these creatures being put through their paces in a hall in London.

'Very second class excursion!' shouted Mildew Turmut. 'We don't get fleas in the trains now only in the holiday season when folks bring their dogs into the carriages. Defraudin' the railways, I call it. They buys dog tickets, but they don't think o' buying tickets for the dog fleas.'

It was an interesting idea, but Robin did not want to argue because he was anxious to show off his own knowledge.

'I mean,' he said, 'I mean performing fleas are trained to pull carriages.'

'Engines pulls carriages!' snorted Mildew Turmut, and Earthy murmured, 'Poor little things: they must need comfortin' arter all that work.'

'We was readin' a book at school,' announced Upsidaisy. 'The childers was readin' it while I did the listenin' outside the winders. It was about places in Africky an' it said as all animals was best shown off in their natural surroundin's. Hens is the natural surroundin's for fleas.'

'Ooh aye!' agreed Gummidge. 'Them and hedgehogs.'

The conversation had made Marlene (because her mother kept hens) feel so tickly that she tried to scratch the difficult place between her shoulder blades. At once the elephant, who had lumbered up unnoticed, scratched it for her with the toe of Worzel Gummidge's bottle-straw boot. Then, very politely, he lowered his trunk, and handed the foot-wear back to the scarecrow.

'Mr Gummidge were doin' a bit o' diggin',' remarked Earthy. 'You casn't dig easy in boots.'

The elephant, who seemed to understand every word that was spoken, slid its trunk along the grass, rootled under Aunt Sally's flowery skirt, and dragged out a black cash box.

The box was earthy and grass-stained, but the words BILTONG'S CIRCUS, printed in white letters, showed clearly enough, as the elephant pushed it towards Gummidge.

'We've been guessin' what's inside of it,' said Earthy. 'Ever since Mr Gummidge dug it up with his foot, we've been guessing what's inside. I'm afeared it's some inseck as wants to get out an' be comforted. You casn't comfort poor soft insecks inside o' hard boxes.'

Hannah Harrow spoke for the first time.

'Most like it's full o' the infections – rust and blight and thrush an' all sorts.'

'There were a terrible disease as we learned about in hist'ry,' announced Upsidaisy cheerfully, 'it were called the plague.'

Instantly Earthy Mangold broke into a flood of green tears, and looked at Worzel Gummidge's coal-black face.

'Oh, Upsidaisy, love, has Mr. Gummidge got that?'

Hannah Harrow crawled away hurriedly, and Mildew Turmut told her own guess, 'There's bank robberies inside.'

'Don't be ridiculous!' snapped Aunt Sally, 'bank robbers are full-sized humans. No human could get into that sized box.'

Mildew flapped her red flag furiously.

'There were a box like that put in the Lost Luggage at Lunnon station, and the man as put it there dropped the left-luggage ticket when he were bein' chased by the perlice, and when the perlice opened the box it were full o' bank robberies. The man as had put it there were a bank robber.'

'Do you mean he'd stole moss and bits o' twigs from banks?' asked Earthy Mangold.

'We know what's in it,' said Robin, but he did not have a chance to tell them because Upsidaisy spoke importantly.

'I knows there's eddication in that box. They bring one to school every now and again, and it's stuffed with exam paper, and when they're give out to the childers they sits down and writes the answers.'

'What answers?' asked Worzel Gummidge.

'They writes the answers to the questions that's writ in the exam papers. It's very eddicatin' accos then the teachers knows what the childers knows.'

'Stands to reason they does if the childers is so daft as to write an' tell 'em the answers.'

'The teachers knows the answers *afore* the childers writes 'em,' explained Upsidaisy. 'The teachers wants to know what the childers knows.'

Earthy looked puzzled, and murmured, 'It do seem complicate – complicate and interferin'.'

'Stands to reason it's daft!' shouted Gummidge. 'And it's not fair neither. If everythink knowed what everythink else knowed, there'd not be many dinners. If early birds knowed as worms knowed they was watchin' the wormholes, they'd not to go on watchin' the worm-holes, and they'd not get no dinners!'

'*We* know what's in the box,' said Marlene.

'*I* know what's in the box,' Worzel Gummidge told her. 'Stands to reason, I knows – else I wouldn't a dug it up. There's *nothin'* in the box – else I'd not a wanted it. Folks put things in boxes. I'd not demean mesel to want a box as'd been put-into by other folks. I wants to put things in mesel. Stands to reason!'

His pink turban was askew over his turnipy face, and his broomstick arms stretched out triumphantly.

'What sort o' things do you want to put in the put-in-box, Worzel love?' asked Earthy Mangold.

'What I've a mind to. It might be a fly if I'd a spite agin a spider. T'otherways on, it might be a spider if I'd a mind to let the fly have a fly-about. It might be one o' Earthy's bottle-straw boots.'

A proud expression came over Earthy Mangold's face. She clasped her twiggy fingers together, and hopped about as she tried to shake off her boots.

'Oh, Worzel, LOVE!' she said, 'you'm welcome to me bottle-straws.'

Instantly, the elephant stopped pushing the cash box about, picked up Gummidge's lost boot, and gave it to him again. While the scarecrow took it, Robin had a chance to speak.

'There's money in that box, and it belongs to the circus people.'

'And you better give it back to them,' added Marlene.

While this conversation had been taking place, the Fat

Lady had left her empty saucepan by the primus stove. Followed by Mr Biltong, she walked across the recreation ground, and came to a stop just opposite to the, now, very sulky-looking Worzel Gummidge.

The elephant lowered its trunk, and pushed the cash-box towards her.

'There now!' exclaimed Mr Biltong. 'I told you I'd left it by the elephant!'

Very slowly and very carefully, because she found it so difficult to bend, the Fat Lady stooped down, picked it up, and shook it.

'It sounds all right,' she said as the coins clattered about. 'The lock's not been tampered with.'

'I knew I'd find it, ducks, if you'd only give me time.'

Mr Biltong stopped looking like a disgraced puppy, and pushed his hat to the back of his head.

'Beggin' your pardon, and if it's all the same to you,' said Earthy, 'it were my husbin', Mr Gummidge, as dug it up, an' broke his boot on it.'

The Fat Lady looked very put out as she turned to whisper wheezily in her husband's ear, 'That means they expect a reward. You'd better unlock the box, and give them some money. I suppose you've got the key?'

Mr Biltong did not look as though he had the key. His mouth turned down at the corners, and a network of frowns showed on his forehead, as he began to turn out his pockets, shaking the linings in a despairing sort of way.

'Money!' repeated Worzel Gummidge. 'Money's daft. Mrs Braithewaite gives Mrs Kibbins money arter she's scrubbed the dairy floor, and Mrs Kibbins takes the money to Dimden and buys some twisted-up straw with a mock rose on it, and puts it on her head. She could twist up some straw herself and put a proper rose on it without scrubbin' the dairy floor first, and then sayin' her knees hurts. I'd not demean mesel with money. I takes what I wants when I wants it. Even pigs isn't daft enough to go hurryin' to Dimden to buy plaited-up straw with roses on it – nor's centipedes daft enough neither.'

'Money is the root of all evil!' snapped Aunt Sally.

'Money's very complicate,' agreed Earthy Mangold, 'I wunner how them little money spiders manages?'

Mr Biltong looked a little more cheerful, though his last pocket was quite empty, its lining flapping against the side of his coat.

'Do you mean to say you don't want any money?' asked the Fat Lady.

'Stands to reason I'd not demean mesel.'

Worzel Gummidge spoke very proudly indeed.

'Beggin' your pardon,' said Earthy, 'beggin' your pardon, an' if it's all the same to you, we're goin' to set up a circus with oursels, so we'll not be stayin' along o' you, beggin' your pardon, and if it's all the same to you.'

The Fat Lady's face creased into plump wrinkles of pleasure. She put her huge hands on her enormous hips, and rocked to and fro with laughter.

'Well, I never did!' she cried, and the tears streamed down her cheeks, 'and there was me and Biltong wondering how to tell you that we're moving on, and shan't be needing you any more.'

'That's right, ducks! Laugh and grow fat!'

Mr Biltong nodded happily as he tucked the linings of his pockets back into place.

'So you're starting your own circus,' continued the Fat Lady. 'As soon as I set eyes on you, I said to myself, "those folks are in show business: they look *different.*" I'll say one thing, old Ali Gummidge is a rare elephant trainer when he puts his mind to it.'

8 The Beginning of a Circus

It was Tuesday morning. In the time between sleep and waking – that queer bit of time when dreams mingle with the knowledge that yesterday has changed miraculously into today – Robin decided that he would get up at five o'clock, rush to the recreation ground, and say good-bye to the Fat Lady and Mr Biltong.

'I'll get up in ten minutes,' he told himself.

But, long before ten minutes could have gone by, it was six o'clock by the big watch under his pillow.

'I'll get up at seven,' he thought. 'I'll keep the watch *out*, and then I'll keep hearing the ticks.'

In no time at all it was eight o'clock.

So Marlene, whose bedroom looked out on to Scatterbrook village street, was the one to see Biltong's Circus moving in a long procession towards Penfold.

The merry-go-round had been hoisted on to a flat dray. The Big Top had been stowed under canvas. Sulkily, very sulkily, the elephant, with Pick-me-up on top, followed a piebald pony. The lurcher dog trotted under the wheels of a caravan, driven by the Fat Lady, who was shaking like a jelly because the road was bumpy. The sea-lions roared in their cages. The boy who looked after the merry-go-round, chatted to Mr Biltong as they walked along together.

So, with a creaking of wheels, and in a flurry of dust, mingled with all manner of queer smells, Biltong's Circus left the village of Scatterbrook.

Marlene had seen its departure, and Robin had not. She boasted about it in the school playground.

'I heard the sea-lions,' she told him.

'I don't care if you heard sea-elephants or sea-horses!' snapped Robin.

He was cross, partly because it had been so silly not to get up when he was awake – or very nearly awake; partly because he knew he was going to miss the elephant very badly indeed, and partly because the string of Finch Cottage key was sawing the back of his neck. Until now, he had forgotten that it *was* there. He ought to have hidden it because this was the morning when Miss Dollit might keep her threatened promise. What should he do if she came prancing into the school-room, and insisted on taking Mr Kimber to see the scarecrow pictures?

'I can turn out my pockets,' thought Robin, remembering Mr Biltong, 'I can show the key's not *there*.'

'You might *listen*!' said Marlene, interrupting his thoughts. 'You might *look*! I found *these* caught in the hedge: they're elephant hairs!' She held out a straggle of long, wiry black hairs.

'Horse-hairs!' snapped Robin.

As a matter of fact, the hairs had come from the tail of Winny, Farmer Braithewaite's pony mare, but neither Marlene nor Robin knew this. Had he been in a nicer mood, he would have let her go on thinking the best; but he was feeling worried.

'They were there after the elephant left,' persisted Marlene. 'It *might* have scratched against the hedge. Are you coming to see *their* circus tonight – the scarecrow one?'

She could not have said anything more tiresome! Of course Robin could not go to the Scarecrow Circus. He must, unless Miss Dollit spoiled everything, try to rub out the drawings on Finch Cottage walls. Marlene had *said* she would help.

Luckily the school bell rang.

It was *not* a good morning for Robin. He kept looking at

the school-room door when he should have been looking at the blackboard, and looked at it so often that Mr Kimber threatened to keep him in after school unless he paid attention.

The 'Art' class began, and Robin, who *should* have been drawing a chestnut leaf from memory, doodled spiders' webs all over his nice white paper.

There came a thump on the door.

'Now for it! Now for Miss Dollit!' thought Robin, and broke his pencil.

In came Mr Lane, the Scatterbrook painter and decorator.

'Sorry to intrude,' he said, 'I went to the policeman first, but he was out, and his mother said I'd better find Robin Elliot.'

The broken wood of Robin's pencil stabbed into the paper, and Mr Kimber beckoned to him.

'I want the key of Finch Cottage,' went on Mr Lane. 'Mrs Bolton said I was to give the walls and floors a good scrub down before I started whitewashing all over. I've not all that time, else I wouldn't have interrupted. We've got the distemper mixed so it shouldn't take all that long. Mrs Bolton said I'd find it in a rare mess, but we'll get over that.'

His Aunt Ruby's idea of a 'rare mess' meant no more than a shadowy mark or so where a picture had been hung, but Mr Lane was used to all sorts of cottages. Everything would be all right now.

Everything was made even more all right by Mr Lane's next words.

'I met that Miss Dollit in the school yard. She said she'd a fancy to look over the cottage, but I told her we'd got to get on, and she'd best keep out of the road of our brushes if she didn't want to get spattered with distemper.'

Thankfully, Robin unhitched the string from round his neck, and handed the key over.

'Thanks,' said Mr Lane, and added, 'Miss Dollit wasn't best pleased, but we've got our work to do.'

Robin drew quite a good chestnut leaf on the other side of the paper.

Now he would be able to go to the Scarecrow Circus. Everything was very much all right. He felt that he could scarcely wait until after tea.

He was not, because his Uncle Dick had decided to cook a 'real meal', and had let the fire go down to a few cinders and some bits of damp wood, able to leave Scatterbrook station until nearly six o'clock.

Mildew Turmut was waiting outside the recreation ground. The rope barrier had been taken away, but she was striding up and down like a sentinel.

'Tickets please! All tickets ready!' she shouted.

'I don't need tickets for this – it isn't a proper circus,' argued Robin.

Certainly, the recreation ground looked very deserted. A few tins and bottles, pieces of torn tarpaulin and packing cases were strewn about.

A canvas screen had been left standing, and in front of it stood Aunt Sally. Her pipe was in her mouth, and her flowery skirts were fluttering in the wind. There was no other movement from her, and she looked like a perfectly ordinary and well-behaved Aunt Sally – the sort who may be seen at garden fêtes on vicarage lawns.

Not very far from her and just at the entrance to a clump of elder bushes, a party of three picnickers – a man, a woman, and a little boy – were carrying rugs and baskets from a motor-car.

'All tickets, please,' repeated Mildew. 'Mr Gummidge said you was to have tickets for the feedin' time.'

'But,' said Robin, remembering one glorious day at Regent's Park, 'but this isn't the Zoo. The sea-lions and the elephant went this morning, and there aren't any lions or tigers.'

Marlene, very breathless, came running up in time to hear Mildew Turmut's explanations.

'It'll be Human feedin'-time soon. There they are, look!'

Mildew waved her red flag towards the picnickers. 'Cheap-day-trip-excursion – sort! Special-rates-for-large-parties. Crumbs-on-the-seat. Breath-and-sticky-fingers-on-the-window-panes!'

'Come on!' said Marlene, as the railway scarecrow continued her patter.

The two children charged across the recreation ground. They were in too much of a hurry to notice where they were going, and pulled up only just in time to avoid bumping into Aunt Sally.

'Sorry!' gasped Robin.

Aunt Sally jerked up a hand, and took the pipe out of her mouth.

'Good evening! You have not grown much since last I saw you.'

Marlene answered pertly, 'The school doctor says we're a very good height for our age.'

'That is not grammatical – nor is it true. You should say – "We are very poor heights for our *ages*".'

'But Dr Smithson—' began Marlene again.

Aunt Sally pursed up her lips, and jerked the pipe back into her mouth, as though to show that the conversation was ended.

It was just as well because before the children could move away, the woman picnicker came up with the little boy.

'Where *is* this circus?' she asked.

'It's here,' answered Robin, 'sort of.'

Then he wished he had not spoken because the woman began to complain, and to ask questions. She said she had seen a notice in the village, and had been directed to the recreation ground. Why, she asked, had money been taken by a ticket collector when there were no roundabouts or swing-boats or animals or side-shows?

'There *was* an elephant,' said Marlene rashly. 'I've got some of its hairs to sell: they're ever so lucky.'

She held out some of the hairs from Winny's tail.

'I'll sell them for sixpence – a shilling each.'

'Do you belong to the circus?'

'Yes,' said Marlene because she *had* been asked to come to the Gummidge's Circus.

'Is that person who took money from us,' the woman pointed to where Mildew Turmut was waving her red flag, 'is that person who took money from us your mother or aunty?'

'No,' giggled Marlene, waving her horse hairs at Aunt Sally, 'no, but this one's my aunty!'

'You are a bad, wicked little girl!'

The woman's angry words startled Robin, who had been looking at the small boy, and deciding he did not like him.

'You are a bad, wicked little girl to tell such stories, and to try to sell me common horse hairs for a shilling each.'

The voice of Hannah Harrow rose in the distance.

'Cutall's Kill-All kills dullness and rust.'

'It sounds as though something's beginning,' said the woman (her name was Mrs Stubbs). 'We may as well see what we can see, after paying. Come on, Eddie!'

But Eddie Stubbs was collecting sticks and stones and bits of broken tent pegs to throw at Aunt Sally. Robin watched him joyfully for a moment or two before following the others towards the edge of the spinney on the far side of the recreation ground.

Hannah Harrow was standing behind a packing case littered with bottles and tins left behind by the Biltongs.

She was chanting in her doleful voice:

'What can't be cured
Must be endured,
But find me the ill
That Kill-all can't kill.'

Earthy Mangold looked on admiringly, and Worzel Gummidge was shambling about in the background.

'I suppose she's some sort of quack doctor,' remarked Mrs Stubbs. Hannah Harrow waved a tin that had once held machine oil.

'I'm a lady doctor,' she wailed. 'I kill more nor quacks. I kill Moos and Baas and Barks.'

For fear Mrs Stubbs should misunderstand, the tender-hearted Earthy Mangold explained, 'She don't mean she'd kill cows and sheep and dogs – only the moos and baas and barks, and only for a bit if they was disturbin' dormice that needed their winter naps.'

She patted the grass by her side.

'Come and sit here, love, while we harks at Hannah. I'm glad as you came to our circus. We've some lovely tight-rope walkers. They spins their own ropes from their own stummicks and then they swings from 'em. Lovely silver ropes they spins, too. You'd never think they could spin 'em so long out o' such fiddlin' little stummicks. Sit aside me, love!'

Mrs Stubbs may have been afraid of sitting on damp grass (not that the grass was damp) or she may have been afraid of sitting next to kind little Earthy Mangold.

Anyway, she moved quickly away from her, and nearer to Hannah Harrow, who shouted, 'Cutall's Kill-All will kill *all* your fleas!'

There was a horrid silence, broken, at last, by Marlene's giggles, and a hissing gasp from Mrs Stubbs.

'Of all the impudence!' she cried, and broke into a teetering run (she had had a long day in the country; her shoes were tight and much too high-heeled) towards the place where her husband was spreading a rug.

Hannah, looking very disappointed, wailed, 'If only she'd a waited, I'd a told her as Kill-All kills the cloths moths, too!'

In the background, little Eddie Stubbs was throwing sticks at Aunt Sally.

Mildew Turmut was striding across the recreation ground.

'Stands to reason, it's time we got on with the circus!' announced Worzel Gummidge.

There isn't any circus left,' said Marlene. 'There's only the old Aunt Sally.'

'There's performin' humans. There's you and him—'

Gummidge pointed one broomstick arm at Robin, and swung the other towards the picnic party, 'An' there's THEM. In a nonery circus you gets animals actin' like humans. I've learned a lot o' circus gossip while I've been trainin' that nelephant. In a nonery circus, you gets monkeys dressed up, and eatin' their teas like humans. and you gets nelephants sittin' about on stools, and you gets sea-lions playin' ball.'

'I thought it were moths as played ball,' interrupted Earthy Mangold.

Worzel Gummidge continued his speech.

'Humans laughs when they sees animals actin' like daft humans: they hasn't the sense to see as the animals is makin' a mock o' them. In my circus, we're goin' to have humans actin' like animals, and then see who'll laugh. Wait till Mrs Kibbins's cat comes along, and sees you set down on all fours to a saucer o' milk!'

A sound of mewing came from the spinney behind Worzel Gummidge. The mews were uttered by Mrs Kibbins's cat, who, tired of a fireless summer hearth, was harking back to the ways of her ancestors, and exploring the best jungle she could find.

'Sea-lions'll roar laughin' when they sees you tryin' to catch fish in your mouths at feedin' time. Humans is a lot more comic nor most animals. You starts bald – most o' you.'

'Humans needs comfortin' when they starts, Worzel, love,' put in Earthy. 'They needs comfortin' to start – same as little bald mices and rabbits and lots o' little birds as hasn't no fluff on 'em.'

'There's lots o' humans ends bald – same as they starts,' said Gummidge.

A yell rang piercingly across the recreation ground.

Robin jumped up, and was just in time to see Aunt Sally hurl a tent peg at young Edward Stubbs, and miss him. It must have been her third shot because the boy, clutching his head and yelping loudly, limped towards the place where his parents were sitting.

Robin followed, though he did not know *why*. He only knew that he must try to stop *something* before something much *worse* happened.

He was too late. By the time he reached the rug and the picnic baskets, Eddie was bawling in his mother's arms.

'That Aunt Sally hit me! She threw back at me!'

Mr Stubbs, a red-faced hearty-looking man, who was munching a well-filled sandwich, looked up.

'Don't make such a song and dance!' he said. 'We stopped here for a quiet picnic. Let's have it quiet, for goodness' sake!'

'How can you, Stan?'

Mrs Stubbs smoothed Eddie's curly hair back from his forehead.

'He's ever such a bruise coming up – quite a lump. Just you feel it. You ought to get the police to put that – that—' she pointed towards Aunt Sally's chintz-dressed back – 'you ought to get the police to do *something*.'

Mr Stubbs took another sandwich, and took his first bite from it.

'Last time I asked the police to do something when you said Eddie had been bitten by a savage dog, the police found out that Eddie had been throwing stones at it.'

Eddie whimpered loudly.

'A proper fool I looked!' said Mr Stubbs.

'She threw back at my leg too!' whimpered Eddie.

Mr Stubbs took another bite, and mumbled through it, 'If she threw back, you must have thrown first, and you shouldn't throw things at women. I've told you that before.'

Robin, remembering Aunt Sally's pinches, did not think Mr Stubbs was being quite fair, but he could not be sorry because he disliked Eddie so much.

'Just look at his poor leg!'

Mrs Stubbs pointed to a very small mark on Eddie's plump knee, and Mr Stubbs looked at his sandwich.

'All tickets ready!' shouted Mildew Turmut.

She had joined the picnic party. So had Worzel Gummidge and Earthy Mangold and little Upsidaisy.

The railway scarecrow waved her red flag, and began to talk, very quickly, in a mixture of 'Railway' and 'Circus'.

'Take your seats for the humans' feeding time. Mind your backs! It is dangerous to throw buns to young human beings . . . Do not feed these humans with grass, hay, linseed cake, pig-swill, dandelions, laying-meal or bird-seed. Mind your backs . . . These animals are dangerous!'

'Stan!' gasped Mrs Stubbs. 'Stop them, Stan! Eddie, come to mother!'

Mr Stubbs took another sandwich, and pushed a bag full of cream buns towards Eddie, who took one in each hand.

'Look at 'em!' said Worzel Gummidge, 'look at 'em fillin' their innards with all sorts o' messy all-sorts. Cows eats clean, and cows eats green, so does horses. Humans eats all colours!'

Mrs Stubbs flung her arms round Eddie.

'Stanley!' she cried, 'Stan, go and fetch a policeman.'

'What for?' asked Mr Stubbs. 'They've as much right to be here as we have. What they say won't hurt us. Don't take any notice.'

The truth was that Mrs Stubbs was extremely fussy. Mr Stubbs had chosen picnic place after picnic place, and none had suited his wife. One was too near a wasps' nest, another was in the shade, another close to a stream that might be dangerous for Eddie.

All the same it was difficult not to take notice of the scarecrows.

'Look at 'em!' repeated Worzel Gummidge, leaning against the bonnet of the car, 'look at the young human eatin' *pink* food!' (Eddie was now sucking a large raspberry-coloured lolly.) 'Anamiles and insecks wouldn't demean 'emselves to eat PINK food – they eats green, and corn coloured and brown.'

'There's some *birds* as eat pink worms, Worzel, love,' put in Earthy.

'Ooh aye! I scares birds. Anyways, birds covers their faces decent with feathers. Human faces is pink acos they eats pink. Very disgustin' human faces is – all acos o' the messed up food they eats. They steals milk from cows and messes it up into butter. They steals corn from fields and messes it up into bread.'

Eddie began to bellow again.

'Savage that one is,' said Gummidge. 'When young human bein's gets savage, they open their mouths and squawks like starlin's.'

'They're mad, Stan!' cried Mrs Stubbs. 'Let's pack up and go away.'

Reluctantly, Mr Stubbs shook the crumbs from his trousers and stood up. Mrs Stubbs bundled cups and saucers into baskets, and threw the paper on to the grass.

Hannah Harrow drifted saggingly towards the group of humans and scarecrows.

She was a most remarkable sight. During the time she had been left alone, she had devoured a packet of soap flakes, and had followed this up (or rather *down*) with several bottles half full of mineral water that had been left behind by the boy who looked after the merry-go-round. The mixture had frothed inside her and oozed out through her sacking skin. Now she was covered with grimy-looking bubbles. They frothed from her mouth as she moaned, 'I've got the cleanin' fever!' and sank on to the rug.

Eddie yelled, and Mrs Stubb's voice was very *nearly* a yell.

'That one's frothing mad! Where have you brought us, Stan? Pick up the rug quickly.'

Tipping Hannah Harrow from the rug's fringed edge, shaking papers and empty tins on to the grass, Mr Stubbs did pick up the rug.

Then he dropped it because Aunt Sally was approaching jerkily.

Robin felt almost sorry for Eddie, who hurled himself at his mother, and screamed, 'That's the one that threw at me!'

The fag end of Mr Stubbs's cigarette was making a tiny fire among some sandwich wrappings. Aunt Sally stamped on it with the foot that belonged to her hinged leg.

'Rise from each meal feeling as though you could eat another one,' she said. 'Do not dig your grave with your teeth.'

'My teeth are all of a froth,' whimpered Hannah.

'Waste of soap!' snapped Aunt Sally. 'Do not leave the soap in the bath water!' She turned to Mrs Stubbs, and shouted 'Leave no litter!'

'Penalty for improper use of litter not exceeding five pounds,' yelled Mildew Turnut, waving her red flag, and fanning the fire into another blaze. Obligingly, Hannah Harrow rolled onto it. There was a fizz and a splutter as the frothing mineral water met the flame, and the fire went out.

Little Upsidaisy came trundling out of the spinney and across the grass. She had a red sock on one leg, a yellow one on the other, and the third one was covered by a wrinkled black stocking.

'Upsidaisy! Upsidaisy!' she said cheerfully. 'I'm the "Two-legged Eddicated Wonder". When it's dusker the black stocking won't show, and folk'll think I'm two-legged.'

'They aren't safe!' Mrs Stubbs clutched her husband's arm. 'Try to find a policeman.'

'Perlice!' said Gummidge scornfully.

'A policeman would say what I say, "Pick up that litter!" '

After making that remark, Aunt Sally again pursed her mouth into a very round O.

'I suppose we'd better humour them,' said Mrs Stubbs.

Then she and her husband and Eddie began to pick up the empty tins and paper and ice-cream cartons, while Aunt Sally gave her bracing orders.

'Keep a stiff upper lip!' (Eddie's was trembling.) 'Keep a straight back!' (That was difficult for Mr Stubbs while he was picking up papers.) 'A stitch in time saves nine!' (Mrs Stubbs was in no mood for sewing.) 'Worzel, don't stand there idling. Help me clear up the litter.'

This was too much for Worzel Gummidge.

'It's *my* circus! If humans wraps up their dinner in papers, let humans pick the papers up. You don't catch cows wrappin' their dinners in paper. Stands to reason.'

'They'd need a lot o' paper, poor things, if they was to wrap up each grass blade,' agreed Earthy Mangold.

'Worzel, do as Aunt Sally tells you!'

'It takes two to make a aunt,' muttered Gummidge. 'You couldn't be a aunt if it wasn't for me.

He backed away, as Aunt Sally advanced towards him, snapping her tweaky fingers.

Mr Stubbs was picking up litter – not the remains of the picnic party now, but things left behind by the Biltongs.

'Since the car has called for me, I shall go for a drive,' said Aunt Sally majestically.

Now the Stubbs's car was the kind that is known as a *station-van*. There was a lot of room in front, and a great deal more in the van part at the back. AND the back doors were open.

Aunt Sally jerked herself towards it, jerked herself into it, and lay down.

Mr Stubbs noticed nothing: with papers tucked under his arms and stuffing his pockets, with his hands full of tins and bottles, he hurried up to the car.

He threw the litter into the back of the car, flung the rug over it, slammed the back doors, and jumped into the driving seat.

'Anything for a quiet life!' said Mr Stubbs as he drove away.

9 The Short Ride Home

It was very quiet on the recreation ground. Yes, it was very quiet indeed.

Worzel Gummidge, Robin and Marlene were running. Earthy Mangold hopped, Upsidaisy trundled, Mildew Turmut strode, and Hannah Harrow sagged along *somehow*.

In time, they all came to the stretch of grass at the edge of the trees. An old white hen (she belonged to Mrs Kibbins) was scratching about in an aimless sort of way.

Grey in the twilight, the spokes of a spider's web clung to the twigs of an elder-bush. The spider sat in the very middle of the web.

'That's the tight-rope walker,' whispered Earthy Mangold. 'It spun the rope from its stummick.'

'There's the performin' fleas!'

Worzel Gummidge pointed his broomstick arm towards the hen, who scratched herself obligingly.

'Let 'em stay in the nat'ral surroundin's!' Upsidaisy looked down at her black-stockinged leg. 'They'm best seen in their nat'ral surroundin's, and that's hen feathers. It says so in eddication.'

Suddenly Marlene shivered.

'I wish I'd a fur coat,' she said, 'I wish I'd a fur coat like Aunt Emily's one.' She plumped down on the grass and pulled the hem of her blue cotton frock over her bare knees. 'No, I don't want a fur coat *just* like Aunt Emily's. I'd like a *live* fur coat just for *now* without hurting anything.'

'That's easy, love,' whispered Earthy Mangold. 'That's easy as anything.'

Robin wished he had a moleskin waistcoat – the sort the keeper wore under the coat with the big pockets.

Like Marlene, he did not want anything to be hurt, though he would like to be warm.

Everything, thought Robin, everything was lucky. The walls of Finch Cottage were being distempered. His parents were coming to Scatterbrook. Aunt Sally had gone. There had *been* a circus. Another circus was happening.

A lovely warmth crept over him – a living warmth that was spreading where his waistcoat would have been, had he worn a waistcoat. He touched it, and the close warm fur of a living mole trembled under his hand.

'I've a *live* fur coat!' cried Marlene.

So she had. The little pink paws of the moles patted each other's fur as they stole about her, and turned every gap of chill into a breathing warmth.

'I said it were easy!' whispered Earthy.

'Circuses!' said Worzel Gummidge. 'Circuses is daft!'

Robin agreed with him.

Mildew Turmut blew her whistle and announced 'I'll be gettin' back to train-scarin' on the railway allotment.'

'Earthy and me'll be up at Ten Acre Field soon as harvest's in,' said Worzel Gummidge. 'Ooh aye! Stands to reason.'

He stretched up a broomstick arm and snatched the pink turban from his head.

'Oh, Worzel, LOVE!' cried Earthy.

She picked up the veil in twiggy fingers, and laid it gently over her potato-sprouting hair. 'I can't tell you how I've missed my veil!'

'I'm tired o' bein' a nelephant trainer,' said Worzel Gummidge.

Bending his head, he rubbed it against Hannah Harrow's frothy shoulder. Soot joined the soap bubbles. Soon the scarecrow's face was clean. Well, nearly clean.

'I ought to go home,' said Marlene. 'Mum's at a meeting. She doesn't know I'm out. I ought to get back to bed.'

Her fur coat scattered into hundreds of living moles, and pit-pit-pattered away over the grass.

Robin was alone. The scarecrows were gone, too.

The voice of Mrs Kibbins's cat rose from the spinney.

Then came the sound of a squeaking wheel and the sound of Uncle Dick's voice:

'There you are, lad. Mrs Bloomsbury-Barton asked Bert to collect her Aunt Sally. He wanted to go to the pictures, so I said I'd fetch it. I reckon the circus folks must have taken it along with them, so you can have a ride home. In you get!'

In Robin got – into the wheel-barrow – as his moleskin waistcoat went on its many ways.

'I reckon it doesn't matter all that much,' said Uncle Dick, as he picked up the barrow handles. He meant that Aunt Sally did not matter.

'Nothing,' thought Robin, 'nothing matters except Scatterbrook and the scarecrows.'

He was asleep before he reached Station Cottage, and so he did not see Mildew Turmut flapping her flags at an elephant hawk moth.